"There are only three things that America will be remembered for 2,000 years from now when they study civilizations: the Constitution, jazz music, and baseball. They are the three most beautiful things this culture has ever created."
—Gerald Early, American poet, essayist, and college professor, in an interview for Ken Burns' acclaimed PBS baseball filmography released in 1994.

Cover art by author, who never owned the most prized Topps baseball card, but was pleased with the opportunity to draw it.

Baseball Is The Greatest Game

A thesis by

Ted Field

authorHOUSE

AuthorHouse™
1663 Liberty Drive
Bloomington, IN 47403
www.authorhouse.com
Phone: 833-262-8899

Published by AuthorHouse 09/19/2024

ISBN: 979-8-8230-3343-5 (sc)
ISBN: 979-8-8230-3342-8 (e)

Library of Congress Control Number: 2024918638

Print information available on the last page.

A Thesis by Ted Field

"This ain't football. We do this every day."
—Earl Weaver, ex-Baltimore Orioles Manager

"You spend a good piece of your life gripping a baseball and in the end it turns out that it was the other way around all the time."
—Jim Bouton, ex-Major League pitcher and author

"In baseball, fans catch foul balls. In football, they raise a net so you can't even catch an extra point."
—Thomas Bowell, author, from *The Heart Of The Order*

"Baseball's time is seamless and invisible, a bubble within which players move at exactly the same pace and rhythms as all their predecessors. This is the way the game was played in our youth and in our fathers' youth, and even back then—back in the country days— there must have been the same feeling that time could be stopped."
—Roger Angel, author

"Serendipity is the essence of both games, the writing one and baseball."
—A. Bartlett Giamatti, Former Major League Commissioner

"It ain't over 'till it's over."
—Yogi Berra, ex-player and baseball sage

Contents

1

Top Of The First

"This is some kind of game, isn't it?"
—Cincinnati's Pete Rose, to Boston's Carleton
Fisk, 1975 World Series, Game 6, 10th inning

This book is a thesis. A thesis tries to prove something, or introduce original thought, or both. It attempts to advance an argument about a specific point, and the case I wish to advance in this thesis is that baseball is the greatest game of all.

By greatest, I don't mean most popular. Great and popular aren't necessarily the same. After all, Americans don't have a reputation for the highest taste. But if there was a debate between baseball—our greatest game—and football—reportedly our most popular—over which sport should be declared the National Pastime, baseball would have such an unbeatable lead by the debate's second round the judges could go home. But, of course, there is no such thing as an unbeatable lead in baseball—*"It ain't over 'til it's over,"* as Yogi Berra said—and the remaining rounds would be played anyway to give the football debaters a hopeless chance of catching up. If their side had been ahead in the late rounds, they would have tried to run out the clock.

And with that, I make the first point of my thesis.

Baseball's 1969 World Series was a classic. The Series pitted the heavily favored Baltimore Orioles against the Cinderella New York Mets. But after the Series' first four games, two of which were played in Baltimore's unfriendly Memorial Stadium, the Mets led three games to one and were a single win away from a stunning upset and their first championship. In Game 5,which was played in New York, the Orioles took a 3-0 lead into the late innings and appeared to have the game won. But the Mets tied the score in the 7th and scored twice in the 8th to secure a 5-3 victory and the crown.

In his postgame interview Oriole manager Earl Weaver was asked if he hadn't thought the Orioles would hold onto their lead late in the game and bring the series back to Baltimore where they could win Games 6 and 7.

"You can never do that in baseball," Weaver replied. "You can't sit on a lead and run a few plays into the line and just kill the clock. You've got to throw the ball over the plate and give the other man his chance. That's why baseball is the greatest game of them all."

There is no clock in baseball. Its games are not measured by time. Theoretically, a game can last forever, with both teams given an equal number of outs. In that way, the game is highly democratic. It means that no lead is so great the losing team can't come from behind and win. *It ain't over 'til it's over,"* means that in the absence of a clock the game is played until somebody wins. Yogi was brilliant. He and Earl were saying the same thing, that a team doesn't lose any of its allotted 27 outs just because time ran out.

This thesis isn't just about the major leagues; it's about baseball played at any level. The game's gifts are felt at every level. I once listened to a football fan complain that baseball was boring, its games were too slow, and there was a lot of standing around with nothing going on. My reply was football has *too much* standing around. After completing a play that lasts four to five seconds, football players go into secret huddles for the next twenty. I referred to columnist George Will's famous line. "Football combines the two worst features of modern American life: violence punctuated by a committee meeting."

Then I got serious. I said baseball is *not* slow. It is a *leisurely* game played with interludes of explosive speed. Stolen bases and triples are two of the most exciting things to watch in all of sports. The leisure leaves time for contemplation and analysis. In between baseball's action moments important decisions are being made by every player on the field and a curious fan can lean forward in his seat and speculate what they are. What kind of pitch will the pitcher throw? Why is the right fielder playing where he is? Is the batter going to bunt to advance the baserunners? There is suspense and anticipation as the pitcher comes to his stretch before delivering every pitch.

When a batter puts a ball in play, everything happens at once. But—and here's another reason why the game is the greatest—the fan takes it *all* in. He follows the ball and traces what every player involved in the play does. The outfielder chases after it. The runners round the bases. The pitcher backs up third base. The fan sees the *entire* play from start to finish without missing any of it and when it is over knows exactly what happened and why it happened because he was able to understand it all. The pitcher hung a curve. The outfielder missed the cutoff man. The third base coach waved a runner to a certain death at home plate. The fan saw all of this.

There's a lot going in football but its fans aren't privy to it. After a football play is over and twenty-two guys pull themselves up from a pile, fans can't tell why the play turned out as it did. They *think* they can. But unless they're sitting at home in front of their TV with a color analyst and instant replay to show them what they missed, they really don't know. Football *has* to be watched on TV if a fan is to understand what happened. If you don't believe me, then answer this: when a football coach answers a reporter's question after a game by saying, "I won't know until I see the films", where does that leave the fan?

Baseball is best enjoyed in person, at a ballpark under a bright sun and blue sky or at night under the lights with the entire playing field in view.

There's beauty in baseball. A double play is the most graceful thing to watch in any team sport. It's ballet, with the infielder pirouetting in a leap over second base to avoid a hard sliding runner and fire a bullet to first to double up the batter by a half-step.

The game is hard. Its best hitters fail seven times out of ten. The ones that go 3-for-10 for a career are in the Hall Of Fame.

In *Bull Durham,* one of the best baseball movies, Crash Davis, the journeyman catcher played by actor Kevin Costner, says it best when he tells his minor league teammates, "You know what the difference between hitting .250 and .300 is? It's 25 hits. Twenty-five hits in 500 at-bats is 50 points, OK? There's six months in a season. That's about 25 weeks. That means if you get just one extra flare a week, just one, a gork, a ground ball —a ground ball with eyes—you get a dying quail, just one more dying quail a week and you're in Yankee Stadium."

Major League ballparks are revered like European cathedrals. Fans are attracted to them as much as they are to the game itself. Several years ago I took a road trip with two friends to worship a few. We went to watch games in Detroit, Chicago, and Milwaukee, chosen not just to see the Tigers, Cubs, and Brewers play, but to see *where* they played.

Baseball parks possess unique features to appreciate. The features define them. Fenway Park has a leftfield wall that comes with a name. Wrigley Field has ivy-covered walls. The old Yankee Stadium that Crash spoke of had a short rightfield porch so close to home plate pitchers threw to lefthand batters in paralyzing fear. And Detroit's Tiger Stadium was special because of an oddity it possessed: an upper deck that completely encircled the playing field, holding in the game and all its sounds, and shadows in the afternoon, and home runs. Since the upper deck was added in 1922, only ten players hit home runs that cleared Tiger Stadium's outfield roof and landed in the street outside, including Mickey Mantle, whose blast of 600 feet is believed to be the longest home run ever hit in a Major League game.

Detroit's second deck overhung the playing field in places, offering extraordinary seating. One was directly behind home plate, where the front rail was so close to the field that fans seated there looked *down* on the batter and catcher. Another was in rightfield where seats overhanging the outfield caught flyballs and turned them into homeruns. While I was there, I moved around and sat in both sections to confirm how special the two vantage points were.

Tiger Stadium was old and came with a heritage: it was where baseball legends Ty Cobb and Al Kaline had played. But the stadium was to be torn down and replaced after the season was over, so my friends and I went there as a pilgrimage to pay our last respects. Milwaukee's County Stadium was included in our itinerary for the same reason. Wrigley Field? *C'mon.* It's Wrigley Field. *What other reason did we need?*

I've never heard a football fan say, "I have to go see a game in

Soldier Field. It's so special and Walter Payton played there." Football stadiums are football stadiums. Artificial turf is artificial turf. Nothing distinguishes one playing field from another. They are rectangles of the same dimensions. Goal posts are the same everywhere. They only differ with respect to what is painted on the turf in the end zone in front of them. Football doesn't have a single stadium to compare with Wrigley Field.

All ballparks, even the small ones where amateurs play, have their uniqueness. Upon arriving a fan will stop to note what they are, not just for eye pleasure, but because he knows they may impact the game he is about to see. He examines the dugouts, the scoreboard, and the bullpens. He looks at the flag to see if the wind is blowing and in what direction. If it's a minor league or townball park he will read the mural of ads from local businesses on the outfield walls. He notes how far away the walls are, too, because their distance—like the wind direction—will affect the game. So will the foul territory—yes, *foul* territory—because unlike football's out of bounds, baseball is played outside its foul lines. A ball crossing a foul line from an errant throw is still in play and must be chased down. A whistle doesn't blow to tell players to stop what they're doing.

Pitchers prefer ballparks with lots of foul territory because pop fouls are more likely to be caught for outs than reach the seats. There has never been a football field where defenses were helped by sidelines pushed closer together.

No other sport has a treasure chest of quotes, anecdotes, and stories about its most famous players like the one baseball keeps. They speak to what is special about the game and I turn to many of them in this book to support my thesis.

Baseball fans are comforted by the game's timeless rituals and sameness. They cherish the familiar. The green grass and the brown fan of infield dirt. The rise of the mound. The white chalk lines and bases ninety feet apart. It's a ritual before every game to chalk the batter's box and base lines. The lines aren't permanent like the painted lines on a football field. Chalking them is part of the game's leisure, a sacred rite and connection to the game's past and games played everywhere.

Before a game umpires and coaches meet at home plate to go over the ground rules because they differ from field to field. They don't meet to flip a coin because home teams *always* invite their guests to bat first. The pre-game ritual would be missed if ground rules were printed and handed out in private. It is too important not to be given a ceremony and serves as a familiar prolog to a game, like the prelude before a church worship. There's a ritual hymn, too, *Take Me Out To The Ball Game*, sung while fans stretch in the 7th inning. Football fans don't stand up to sing after the 3rd quarter. They rush to the restrooms.

The game's history is linked with the nation's. For years the Washington Senators hosted presidents at their season openers. From President Taft in 1910 until 1971—when the Senators left for Texas—presidents were 45 for 62 throwing out first balls on Opening Day. No president ever received an invitation to throw a pass before a football game.

Baseball has a creation story set in a small town named after a classic American author. The story includes an Army general who would become a hero in the nation's Civil War. But the game has an evolution story, too, one that starts in the nation's largest city with businessmen devising a weekend game that one day they would take across the Hudson River to play, and in doing so contribute not only to the development of the National Pastime but to the westward expansion that defined the nation at the time.

The histories of small towns everywhere include their own semi-pro or amateur teams.

The life story of the game's greatest hero, Babe Ruth, is told in the context of his excesses and those of his era, the Roaring '20's. Twenty years later the major leagues struggled to survive as many of its players went off to war. And when the nation was ready to step forward on its long march to civil rights, Jackie Robinson took the lead, out front breaking baseball's color barrier long before Martin Luther King came on the scene.

In the Korean War Ted Williams, baseball's greatest hitter, was a pilot and wingman for future astronaut John Glenn. And when the

Communist red scare swept the nation in the 1950's, the Cincinnati *Reds* changed their name to the *Redlegs*.

Stand-up comedian George Carlin once had a routine comparing baseball to football. He pointed out the language differences of the two sports. Football was *technical,* while baseball was *pastoral.* Football had *tackles, clips, bombs, and sudden death;* baseball had *sacrifices.* Football was filled with reminders of war. Its players wore *helmets,* while baseball players wore *caps.* The object in football, according to Carlin, was to march downfield and penetrate enemy territory and get into the end zone, sometimes using precise aerial assaults. In baseball, the object was to go *home,* to be safe at home.

Look at home plate and tell me it doesn't look like a little house.

Round One of the debate is over.

2

Baseball Is Life

"It's never fourth-and-one in baseball."
—Earl Weaver, Baltimore Orioles ex-manager

L et's start with something that is beyond dispute. Baseball is the sport that mirrors real life. It matches the seasonal cycles and rituals of our lives.

A baseball season spans the months between spring and fall when we're outside engaged in healthy activities and moments of leisure or festivity. It moves through our lives like a pleasant breeze as the *summer* game, never touching winter. It's when our lives are closer, when we see each other more often, at picnics or on vacations, or at parades, fairs, weddings, graduations and other celebrations. We find each other and come together in the summer.

A poet named Donald Hall once said that baseball starts with the promise of spring and ends with the cold hard facts of fall. He could have added that it begins when we plant, a chore done with hope and expectation, and ends when we harvest and our expectations are either realized or dashed.

A ballfield in the off-season resembles an abandoned amusement park. Concession stands are boarded up and empty dugouts are littered with leaves. The chalk lines of the basepaths are washed away. There is a ghostly silence. Donald Hall wrote, "For baseball dies into the October ground as leaves fall, obscuring base path and pitcher's mound…flitting like spooked grounders over second base into the stiffening outfield grass." When winter sets in, a ballfield lies covered by a blanket of untrampled snow, or as Hall said, "The old game waits under the white;

deeper than frozen grass, down at the frost line it waits…to return when the birds return."

At New Year's, while waiting for the birds to return, baseball fans give themselves fresh air studying the off-season trades and free-agent signings. They speculate if their favorite team will improve next season and how the impossible might become possible. By the time the Super Bowl arrives, they're looking at their calendars and counting the days until spring training starts.

When baseball comes back to us, it opens slowly like a flower, one beautiful petal at a time. It starts in February, in the sunshine of Florida and Arizona, where winter never really came, as Major League baseball renews its "promise of spring" by inviting pitchers and catchers to report for pre-season training. By early March exhibition games with full lineups are being played. Up north, as we endure the last days of winter, we read the box scores of our favorite team, not recognizing many of the names. Then, rosters are trimmed and unfamiliar players are given minor league assignments. Finally, when muscles are limber and arms are strong, major leaguers bring their game to us along with warm weather and lengthening days. We rush outside and celebrate Opening Day.

The start of the football season, and basketball's too, don't have any connection to the natural rhythms of life. They are *reversed*. Their seasons are reminders to look back and remember finer days. In those autumn months when skies gray, leaves blow, and temperatures drop, we go out to the garage to check that the snow blower will start. We put up the storm windows and prepare to hunker down and hibernate through the shortened days of darkness ahead. Football and basketball fans go inside to watch their games on TV, or—in the case of football fans—layer themselves in Inuit fashion and sit numbly on icy seats with their hands curled around cups of hot chocolate, not cold beer. Everyone feels a disconnect with life and its allotted pleasures, football and baseball fans alike.

The major league season is pleasantly long. With 162 games played by every team, there is a game to enjoy every day. We are comforted that we can watch a game whenever we want and aren't distressed when we happen to miss one because we were busy doing something else that day.

Before cable TV brought baseball games into our dens, we listened to them on radio while working in the garage or kitchen, or dozing in a hammock, or going somewhere in the car. The familiar voice of our favorite broadcaster was a sound of summer that brought us joy. As a youth, while I played baseball during the day, I listened to games at night on a transistor radio held to my ear on a pillow in my darkened bedroom. The tiny radio pulled in games from faraway, not just Senators' games from across the river in Washington. I would turn the dial slowly until I heard amid the static the quiet hum of a baseball stadium crowd and waited to hear the voice of the broadcaster calling the game I had found. When I recognized him, I knew who was playing. Ernie Harwell meant the Detroit Tigers. Bob Elson was the Chicago White Sox. Harry Carey was the St. Louis Cardinals. I would picture the players performing for them. I didn't need TV. I *saw* games all summer long listening to a radio.

In a season of 162 games winning every day is not critical to a team's success. Slumps are to be expected. The best teams will win only 60% of their games, 90 to 100 in a season. Dropping two or three in a row doesn't come with a warning that the season is lost. There is always a game tomorrow that might be the start of a winning streak.

Players know it's how they play in the long run that determines their team's success, and success results from showing up every day and doing their best. They must play hard in 162 games for the chance of winning 90 to 100. They run out grounders and dive for flyballs in insignificant mid-season games when no one is looking because they never know when their efforts will make the difference in giving their team the slight edge needed to win.

Just like in life.

Which brings me to two baseball quotes—both from the great Joe DiMaggio—that speak to the value of persistence and good work. "You ought to run the hardest when you feel the worst," he once advised a teammate. "Never let the other guy know you're down." Another time, when asked why he played so hard in every game no matter its importance, Joe replied, "There's always some kid who may be seeing me for the first time. I owe him my best."

Baseball is like our everyday jobs. We show up every day. We do our best, even when no one is looking. Maybe we sit out an occasional sick day knowing we'll feel better tomorrow. We get through the days when we're off a little with the same calmness and purpose as our good days. Our careers are defined by what we do in the long run.

A pro football season is only 16 games. Each game is a cauldron of life-or-death circumstances, like brain surgery and moon landings. Gamedays are a week apart and one bad day can be fatal and cost a team its chance to win the championship. Players and fans have to wait a whole week for the redemption needed after a loss. Players wear their *game face* as they play, that mood of mortal crisis that must be put on like a mask. They tense up for every game and are not permitted to loosen up for a single one. It's the same with their fans.

Most of us can't relate to that kind of tension and urgency. We don't get fired from our jobs for having one horrible day at work. Our bosses aren't Monday-morning quarterbacks questioning what we did with our Sunday.

Baseball writer Thomas Bowell had a fondness for Baltimore Orioles manager Earl Weaver, whom he wrote about often. Early in his career he got a chance to interview Weaver in the dugout before a game started. Boswell was appreciative of the celebrated manager giving a young writer his sole attention, answering all his questions and telling stories while seeming to ignore the game he was about to manage. At one point the umpires and rival manager were standing at home plate waiting for Weaver to go over the ground rules and exchange lineups. They stared at him as he continued to sit in the dugout.

"Excuse me," Weaver said to Boswell, hopping up from the bench. "I'll be right back to finish the story."

The anthem was played and the game was about to begin. Bowell tried to apologize to Weaver for taking so much of his time.

Weaver waved him off. "This ain't football," he replied. "We do this every day."

The remark stuck with Boswell. *We do this every day. Playing every day* is baseball's greatest blessing. Consequently, he wrote, baseball has no *game face*. Baseball must be played with a mix of effort and control. Football is played with anger and adrenaline. It has no place for moderation. Weaver gave Boswell a quote to make his point.

"It's never fourth-and-one in baseball," he said.

True. And rarely is it fourth-and-one in life.

Baseball is life.

3

God And Baseball

"For everything there is a season…a time to seek, and a time to lose."

—Ecclesiastes 3:6

The Christian season of Lent usually starts in mid-February about the same time baseball's spring training is about to begin. Like spring training, Lent is a time of preparation for what is to follow, which is Easter, when Christians proclaim joyfully *He Is risen! Hallelujah, He is risen indeed!* Easter also means Opening Day is here, with baseball fans rejoicing *The season is here! Hallelujah, it is here indeed!*

There are baseball writers who find meaning in the game deeper than who won or who lost. They write about the game's *soul*. They will speak of baseball like it's a religion.

Baseball shares a lot in common with religion and Christianity in particular. Bible parables teach us things like sin, redemption, miracles, and curses. We learn about faith, love, and devotion from them. So it is with baseball, which has its own parables on the same subjects. Banning black players from playing in the Major Leagues was baseball's sin. Jackie Robinson was its redemption. In 1914 the Boston Braves became the Miracle Braves when they rose from the dead to win the National League pennant by 10½ games after being in last place at mid-season. The Boston Red Sox—for trading Babe Ruth—and the Chicago Cubs—for refusing to let a goat into a game at Wrigley Field—supposedly were cursed and prevented from becoming champions for almost a century.

Both baseball and religion struggle with their creation theories.

They are challenged by the facts of evolution. Questions persist. Where did baseball come from? Where did *we* come from?

Verses in Genesis give Christians a foundation for their faith in creation. *Then God said, "Let us make man in our image, after our likeness." (Genesis 1:26)* Of course, we know Genesis begins with a baseball creation reference: in the beginning, which has been translated as *in the big inning*.

Christians are believers of a particular creation story that starts with Adam and Eve in the Garden of Eden. When Christians cite this story in the presence of non-believers, i.e, evolutionists, the two sides clash. They may share a common objective of finding truthful answers but there still is unresolvable conflict.

Baseball's origin is also clouded with conflict. Actually, there is no conflict on the subject. The proof is unmistakable that the game *evolved*. But that doesn't stop many baseball fans from holding onto the game's creation story because of its pastoral splendor, romance, and connection with simple values. The creation story is that in the summer of 1839 in Cooperstown, New York—think of the town as baseball's Garden Of Eden—boys from the local Otsego Academy played a game of "town" ball against the Green Select School under a loose set of rules that allowed every struck ball to be fair and in play. One of the Otsego players named Abner Doubleday drew up a set of rules for the game and gave it the name *baseball*. Doubleday went on to become a hero at the Battle of Gettysburg, and, according to the creation story, the game he devised became the National Pastime.

The story is false in that Doubleday was nowhere near Cooperstown in the summer of 1839. He was at West Point. He never claimed to have invented the game. It is doubtful that he ever saw a professional game. Abner Doubleday didn't invent baseball; baseball invented Abner Doubleday. Despite the facts, a hundred years later Cooperstown became the site of the Baseball Hall of Fame and games are played there today on Doubleday Field.

That doesn't mean Abner Doubleday didn't play a role in baseball's *evolution*. During the Civil War, in their moments of rest and leisure, Union troops would entertain themselves playing baseball in one form or another and it's likely General Doubleday enjoyed watching them play. Southern boys reportedly learned the game in Northern prison camps.

What we know about baseball's creation story is that it was concocted many years after the game had evolved and grown in popularity. In 1907—16 years after Doubleday's death—a special commission led by sporting goods magnate and former major league player A.J. Spalding was created to determine baseball's origin. Was it invented in the United States or was it developed from games played all over, including games in England? The commission used flimsy evidence—the claims of one man, a mining engineer named Abner Graves, who went to school with Doubleday—to come up with the creation story, which managed to stick. You could say it was a foregone conclusion. The National Pastime *had* to have come from our nation, and not from a foreign country.

The creation version is a lovely story. It has a place in American folklore as a Genesis. But Walt Whitman wrote something in 1840 that challenges it.

"In our sundown perambulance of late, through the outer parts of Brooklyn, we have observed several parties of youngsters playing base, a certain game of ball. Let us go forth a while and get better air in our lungs. Let us leave our close rooms. The game of ball is glorious."

In truth, for years settlers from Europe had been bringing to the new world variations of games involving bases and balls. Some called their game *base*. Others called theirs *ball*. But games resembling baseball were already here. On their journey to the west coast Lewis and Clark witnessed members of a Shoshone tribe playing a game that involved striking a ball with a club. At the same time similar games were being played in one form or another in schoolyards in the East. Two notable games that had found their way to America from England were cricket and rounders, and it was from modifications of these two games that a third game—baseball—was derived.

Two years after Walt Whitman's observation a group of New York City gentlemen were getting together on weekends to play one version or another of the game. Three years after that, they organized into a team called the New York Knickerbockers and changed many of their game's rules. For example, the Knickerbockers decreed that runners would be tagged or thrown out, not thrown *at*. But space to play in the crowded city was limited and in search of a playing field the team ventured across the Hudson River to Hoboken, New Jersey, where they discovered a vacant grassy area known as Elysian Fields. They laid out a ballfield and it was on that field on June 19, 1846, the first baseball game of record was played under rules we would recognize today, as the Knickerbockers lost to a team of cricket players, 23-1. Today, common belief is that *baseball in America* began that day.

Baseball still likes to think of itself as a pastoral game. The description deepens its roots in American folklore as the National Pastime and suggests the game grew from the country's heartland. The *pastoral* description keeps baseball in touch with its creation story. Creation or evolution, it really doesn't matter. It's okay for a baseball fan to accept both, just as Christians may find a comfortable truth in between the opposing versions of where they came from. If you accept the notion that truths and facts don't always have to agree, or that truths don't have to be based on facts, then baseball's creation story is as truthful as its evolution story. What truths? That it's a beautiful game. That our vision of a perfect ballfield is pastoral. That Walt Whitman was right when he wrote *Let us go forth a while and get better air in our lungs.* Our nation's history is told through stories as much as it is by facts. George Washington didn't chop down a cherry tree, but cherry pie and George's reputation for honesty are part of our nation's foundation. We're a democracy and we show our democracy when we allow both versions of the game's origin to become stitched together into a common story, and it's a good story.

The Knickerbocker players were amateurs who toiled at day jobs in a variety of professions, as insurance salesmen and investment brokers. They included a doctor and a cigar dealer. Their devotion and skills for the game weren't dependent on their professional talents. In 1846 they may have believed that Elysian Fields was the extent of the civilized world and that baseball might not advance any farther beyond it. But ten years later a local sportswriter labeled their game the *National*

Pastime of a growing nation, and in no time, as our civilization spread westward, the game spread with it.

Such it was with Christ's disciples. Among them were fishermen and a tax collector, possibly a farmer and a baker. With their help Christianity would spread rapidly and extend its reach beyond its roots in the Middle East and Mediterranean. Eventually, it would arrive in America, much farther than the disciples could ever have imagined.

One Knickerbocker in particular was Alexander Joy Cartwright, who is believed to be the actual inventor of the new game. Shortly after baseball's famous inaugural at Elysian Fields, Cartwright heard about the gold strikes in California and packed up and headed west to stake his claim to fortune. It took him and his travelling party five months to reach San Francisco, in part because whenever they stopped to rest along the way they taught locals the Knickerbocker version of baseball.

One day Cartwright would sail to Hawaii to start a business and teach the game to islanders there, too. At a place in Honolulu called Makiki Park, he laid out the first baseball diamond in the Pacific. Cartwright died in 1892, and in 1938 the park was renamed Cartwright Park. Babe Ruth attended the christening and visited the cemetery where Cartwright was buried to place leis on his grave.

Cartwright was a disciple. Let's call him that.

For our own amusement, there are other connections to find between the game and the Bible.

Thou shalt not steal. (Exodus 20:15). Johnny Bench would agree.

For everything there is a season...a time to seek, and a time to lose." (Ecclesiastes 3:6).

For he and all who were with him were amazed at the catch. (Luke 5:9). Willie Mays?

And when God told Noah in Genesis 6:14 to *cover it inside and out with pitch*, he was giving Noah advice for building an ark, but baseball has advice for pitchers to paint the inside and outside edges of the plate with their pitches, and not the middle.

And then there's this verse. *"To the one, he gave five talents, to another two, to another one, to each according to his ability."* (Mathew 25:15) The line is included in the parable about a master who left on a journey after giving his servants varying levels of money—or talents—and upon returning discovered that the servants who received two and five talents had invested wisely. He praised the one who had received five talents for being resourceful, for "entering into the joys of his master."

Baseball's position players—i.e., players other than pitchers—are rated according to how well they master five skills, or talents: hitting, hitting with power, running, fielding, and throwing. Only the game's greatest players have excelled in all five skills. They *enter into the joys of baseball fans.* In all of baseball history the number of players acclaimed for possessing all five talents can probably be counted on two hands. Willie Mays, Joe DiMaggio, and Ken Griffey, Jr. immediately come to mind, all three Hall Of Famers. But there have been others. There are others who have used their talents wisely.

But when is a curse actually the result of a sin? When is a curse self-inflicted? *"It is not for a good work that we are going to stone you but for blasphemy."* (John 10:33) Baseball's sin was to ban players of color too long before gaining redemption in Jackie Robinson and opening its doors to everyone. Some teams were slower than others to redeem themselves. Take the Boston Red Sox. They may have felt their playing woes came from the curse of selling Babe Ruth to the New York Yankees in 1919 but forty years later team owner Tom Yawkey, not known for his racial tolerance, vowed to keep his team White while a parade of good Black players became available. He passed on opportunities to sign the likes of Willie Mays, Hank Aaron, and Roy Campanella until it was too late and only average players were left for the taking, like Pumpsie Green, who became the first Black Red Sox in 1959, twelve years after Robinson had joined the Dodgers. In his 5-year career with the Sox, Green hit .246 with 13 home runs.

Christians believe in the forgiveness of sin and the Red Sox were forgiven in 2004 when they finally won a World Series after 86 years of futility. They were blessed that year with players they had acquired through trades, players who had *come from afar,* Curt Schilling and two with the Biblical names of David (Ortiz) and John (Damon).

4

Bonus Babies

"I was pitching against seventh-, eighth- and ninth-graders, kids 13 and 14 years old... All of a sudden, I look up and there's Stan Musial and the likes. It was a very scary situation."

—Joe Nuxhall

Joe Nuxhall was the youngest player ever to appear in a Major League game. He was 15 when he went straight from high school to the Cincinnati Reds' pitching staff in the spring of 1944. Over the winter the Reds had signed Nuxhall intending to let him graduate first but their roster had become so depleted by players going off to war they put Nuxhall in a uniform on opening day after his high school principal had given them permission.

Nuxhall's pitching debut wasn't until June 10th, when he entered a game against the league-leading St. Louis Cardinals in the 9th inning with the Cards leading, 13-0. The Cards were rough on him. After retiring the first batter he faced, Nuxhall gave up two hits, walked five, and threw a wild pitch. He was removed from the mound without finishing the inning and didn't get into another game that year. He was sent down to the minors and played there while completing high school. He spent eight years in the minors before the Reds called him back, staying this time. He pitched in the majors until 1966.

The first line on the back of Joe Nuxhall's baseball card reports his 1944 statistics as: one game, one inning, and an ERA of 45.00. The next line is 1952, when he appeared in 37 games and recorded a respectable ERA of 3.23.

Several players have made the leap from high school to the majors. Unlike Nuxhall, most of them graduated first. But like Nuxhall, nearly all failed to stay in the majors on their first try and were sent to the minors to groom their skills to Major League caliber. The fact they needed grooming was no surprise to their parent clubs. But they knew that many were like Nuxhall and would one day make it back to the majors and thus were willing to be patient with their investment.

In the years just before World War II Major League teams engaged in fierce and competitive bidding for young players. The bidding subsided during the war but resumed after 1945 with skyrocketing signing bonuses given to promising players. Then, in 1947 Major League Baseball enacted a rule called the Bonus Baby Rule that required a team signing an amateur player with a bonus offer greater than $4,000 to immediately assign the player to their big league roster and keep him there for the next two years. Why? The league feared the wealthiest teams would sign all the best players and then stash them in their farm systems. The Bonus Baby Rule was devised to keep the rich teams in check. The rule was challenged several times and for a while in 1950 was rescinded, only to be revived in 1952, then rescinded, and revised again. It ended finally in 1965.

Teams sought ways to circumvent the rule. The New York Yankees, for instance, made a secret deal with the Kansas City Athletics involving a bonus baby named Clete Boyer. The Athletics signed Boyer and then proceeded to play him sparingly for the obligatory two years, but when the two-year obligation ended, instead of sending Boyer down to the minors, they shipped him off to the Yankees as the "player to be named later" from a trade made the previous winter. The owners of other American league teams protested. But the Yankees got away with it and their arrangement with the Athletics was allowed to stand. For years after the Boyer trade the Athletics continued to sell or trade players to New York and earned the disreputation of being a "Triple A farm club" for the Yankees.

As a consequence of the Bonus Baby Rule, nearly all bonus babies started their Major League careers lacking the necessary skills to be there. They were talented, promising players but just needed more time to develop. An example was one of my favorite players growing up as a Washington Senators fan, Harmon Killebrew, who would go to become a Hall of Famer with 573 career home runs, ranked 12th all-time as of this writing. Killebrew signed with a bonus in June, 1954, and four days later was in a Senator's uniform. In his two-year Major League assignment, he scarcely played, hitting only 9 home runs and batting .200. Then, for the next 2 ½ years as a minor leaguer he hit 63 homers in 336 games for the Nats' farm clubs in Charlotte and Chattanooga. He returned to the Senators ready to show off what he had learned and in 1959, his first full year in the majors, tied for the American League home run lead and made the All-Star team.

Killebrew was just one in a wave of bonus babies in the 1950's, a decade in which 24 high schoolers signed major league contracts. Only two of the 24 were good enough to have successful major league careers without ever playing in the minors: future Hall-Of-Famers Sandy Koufax and Al Kaline, although Koufax struggled for a while and could have benefitted from some minor league training. Many of the 24 enjoyed great major league careers, too, but *after* receiving their minor league training.

Besides Koufax and Kaline, there was Bob Feller, the Hall of Fame pitcher who came along before the Bonus Baby Rule. Still in high school in 1936, he signed with the Cleveland Indians and made his major league debut in July in a relief appearance against the Senators. A month later he made his first career start against the St. Louis Browns, striking out the side in the first inning and finishing the game with a complete-game victory and 15 strikeouts, the highest strikeout total ever in a pitching debut. Three weeks after that he fanned 17 in a win over the Philadelphia Athletics, tying the single-game strikeout record previously set by Dizzy Dean. He ended the season with a 5–3 record and returned to his hometown of Van Meter, Iowa, to finish high school. The governor of Iowa greeted him. His outstanding rookie year had made him, according to one baseball writer, "the best-known young person in America, with the possible exception of Shirley Temple". The next year he returned to the Indians and won 9 games. Then his baseball career took off, and in the three seasons from 1939 to 1941 he won 24,

27, and 25 games. He never pitched in the minors and retired in 1956 with 266 careers wins, an incredible total made even more incredible by the fact that after his successful 1941 season he joined the Navy and spent the next 3 ½ years serving his country in World War II.

Koufax. Kaline. Feller. Out of all the great players of their era they were the only ones who didn't need the minor leagues to prepare them for the majors. They were special indeed.

After the Bonus Baby Rule went away, with very few exceptions Major League teams routed *all* their high-school-signees through their farm systems first. Even the most talented kids needed the improvement playing in the minor leagues would give them. The greatest of them wouldn't take long to get promoted to the show. Mike Trout needed two years. So did Ken Griffey and Joe Mauer, both of whom came out of high school possessing what scouts regarded as the most perfect natural batting swings they had ever seen. Some stars got their grooming on college baseball teams and then went straight to the majors, like Dave Winfield, who reported directly to the San Diego Padres after four years at the University of Minnesota.

The point is *the game is hard*. Talent alone isn't enough to be a star in baseball. Even the game's greatest players had a lot to learn before they were ready for the majors. It's been said that hitting a baseball is the hardest thing to do of all sports, and hitting it *well* is rare craftsmanship. And it's true. Major League pitching is merciless compared to the pitching at the lower levels and even a good hitter isn't ready to hammer big league pitchers until he's paid some dues. No players since Kaline and Koufax have reached the top by skipping all the grades on the way up. Maybe Lebron James and Kobe Bryant could get away with it in professional basketball. But it doesn't happen in baseball. Baseball is not that easy.

5

Like Chocolate Pudding

"In baseball, fans catch foul balls. In football, they raise a net so you can't even catch an extra point."
—Thomas Bowell, author,
from *The Heart Of The Order*

There is something calming about holding a baseball. I keep one in the cupholder of my truck and sometimes while I'm driving catch myself turning it over in my hands and fingering its stitches. It's good therapy. I'm convinced it cures me of road rage. The ball of no other sport has the size and feel to make me want to grip it like a baseball will, not a golf ball or a tennis ball or even a football. A baseball looks good in my hand, too.

"You spend a good piece of your life gripping a baseball," former Big League pitcher and author Jim Bouton once said, "and in the end it turns out that it was the other way around all the time."

Whether it's a new one or a used one, or one inked with a famous signature sitting on a trophy shelf, a baseball has special appeal. I might pass on picking up a golf ball I see lying in the grass but never a baseball. I just have to pick it up.

I own a modest collection of signed baseballs. Brooks Robinson. Harmon Killebrew. Bob Feller. And one signed by the players on the Grade 3/4 2006 Mavericks, my son's little league team I coached. It sits on a shelf next to a Ted Williams ball. I brought it brand-new to a team practice many years ago and passed it around with a Bic pen. "Gee, Mr. Field," one of my players asked, "howcum you want my autograph?" "Because, Ben," I replied, "someday, when you're in the show, this ball will be worth a fortune." With his eyes wide and his mind filled by a widescreen dream, Ben wrote his name between the stitches in a handwriting I would bet was neater than his school homework.

In a typical Major League game between 80 and 120 baseballs are used. On the average a ball will get 5 or 6 pitches before it is tossed out. Any ball that strikes the dirt or is hit foul must be replaced, and the pitcher, catcher, or plate umpire can choose at any time when a ball must go. Once when I was at a game I paid attention to the short lifespans of baseballs and noticed that even when a warm-up pitch between innings skips on the ground, the umpire tosses the pitcher a new ball.

Because MLB rules require that every inning start with a new baseball, it's common that players trotting off the field holding the third out will toss the ball to a fan in the stands.

I noticed something else while ball watching. When a ball is cast aside, the batboy gives it to someone in the dugout who then puts it in a box and writes something on a record he is keeping. Then, at a counter on the stadium concourse it is sold at a steep price with other fan memorabilia. The counter case holds more than a dozen used balls and each comes with authentication of the game, inning, and circumstance in which the ball was last used. I once got one as a birthday present. The note inside its plastic case reads: KC at MN, July 01, 2012. Batter— Billy Butler. Pitcher—Francisco Liriano. Top of 5, Pitch in the Dirt. There's a hologram affixed to the ball that I suppose contains the same information.

Fans get to keep foul balls that reach the stands. And home run balls that land in outfield grandstands. Sometimes, if a player's home run is important enough for him to want the ball back, he will give the fan who caught it an autographed ball or something else of value in exchange. Famous home runs balls will have high dollar value and some—Mark McGuires' 70th, Roger Maris's 61st, or Hank Aaron's 755th—were sold for small fortunes.

Some baseballs have value for a different sort of notoriety. A ball signed by Joe DiMaggio and Marilyn Monroe once got $191,000 in a sale. They weren't married long so I guess it may be the only one in existence. And the ball that rolled between Bill Buckner's legs to win

Game 6 for the New York Mets in the 1986 World Series was purchased at an auction for $418,00. I'm curious to know if any Red Sox fan bid against the Met fan who got it.

Perhaps the most peculiar final resting place for a baseball was where the Steve Bartman ball ended up. Bartman was the Chicago Cub fan who interfered with Cub outfielder Moises Alou as he attempted to catch a foul fly in Game 6 of the 2003 National League playoff series against the Florida Marlins. Alou had reached into the first row of grandstands for the ball but came down without it, which bounced off Bartman's hands instead and was picked up by another fan. Alou was furious at having a certain out stolen from his open glove. Had he caught it, the Cubs would have been only four outs away from going to the World Series. The Marlins went on to score eight runs in the inning and won the game. The next night the Cubs lost Game 7.

For his part Bartman earned a place in Cubs history as another curse to go alongside the goat that had been denied entry to Wrigley Field years before. He was threatened by Cub fans everywhere and offered asylum by Florida governor Jeb Bush. Meanwhile, the ball was sold to a group associated with Harry Caray's Chicago restaurant, and in a public ceremony shown on TV was exploded as a sacrifice to the baseball gods, along with an accompanying prayer that the latest curse that had befallen to the Cubs be lifted. The debris from the explosion was collected and boiled in a mixture of water, beer, vodka, and herbs. The steam was then captured and condensed, with the condensate added to a pasta sauce Harry Carey's served its customers.

In no other sport does the *behavior* of the ball affect play as much as in baseball, as pitchers throw with different spins and speed for a purpose. What they can make the ball do has played an exceptional, singular role in the game's development. Since its creation, when pitchers learned that *how* they threw a baseball could make them better pitchers, they have been trying all sorts of ways to doctor baseballs for better spin and movement. First, they spit on them. When spitballs were outlawed, they tried other illegal substances and methods. They cut and scratched baseballs with their wedding rings and belt buckles. They used Emory boards and sandpaper to roughen a ball's surface. Some got caught. Many others were suspected but got away.

Stitches set a baseball apart from the ball used in any other sport. Stitches are everything. Their orientation when a ball is thrown affects its speed and how much it will spin. Spin creates movement. Movement creates deception and deception makes victims out of batters. They hit weak ground balls and lazy pop flies that fielders turn into easy outs. Deception makes everybody's job on the field easier.

A football's laces are insignificant. They're important only to a quarterback when he's throwing a pass and mean nothing to the other 21 players on the field. The exception might be a placekicker who hooks a field goal attempt and then makes the excuse that the laces were facing him when the holder spotted the ball.

Baseballs have a rubber or cork center. The center is wrapped in yarn and covered with two saddle-shaped pieces of natural horsehide or cowhide held together by 108 stitches, the same number of beads on a Catholic rosary according to Annie Savoy in *Bull Durham*. A ball is a little under 3 inches in diameter and weighs just 5¼ ounces.

I have a personal story about the significance of a baseball's weight.

I once took a backpacking trip on the Appalachian Trail in a region where bears were common. Hikers were advised to hang their food at night out of their reach. I was familiar with the routine. First, I was to secure one end of a rope to the food bag. Then, knot the other end around a rock found in the woods. Toss the rock over a tree branch chosen for its height and strength, and after the food bag is pulled up to a safe height, undo the knot and the toss the rock aside. The last step is to secure the food bag hanging twelve feet overhead by wrapping the rope a couple times around the tree trunk.

I wasn't looking forward to repeating this chore day after day on the trail. Past experience had taught me it wasn't always easy to find a rock of the right size and shape, or one that was easy to throw. Sometimes the rock would slip out of the knot as I threw it and sail off into the woods and I would have to search for another one, sometimes with a flashlight. The task could be time-consuming. Was there a better way?

A baseball was meant to be thrown, I thought.

All backpackers are fussy about pack weight but I figured I could accept an extra 5 ¼ ounces in mine. So, before leaving home I screwed a small eye hook into a baseball and secured a rope to it with a permanent knot. On the trail, food hanging became a lot easier. Every night, with the other end of the rope tied to the food bag at my feet, I stood peering up at a tree branch with the tethered ball gripped in my throwing hand. From a stretch I tossed it over the branch and watched it descend on the other side and land with a reassuring thud on the ground. Without untying the rope, I picked up the ball and wrapped it twice around the tree trunk to hold the bag in place. Easy peasy. One throw every night. It never failed.

Major league baseballs get a special treatment before each game.

Lena Blackburne was a Major League player, manager, and coach in the early 20th century. His career started as a player with the Chicago White Sox in 1910 and ended as a coach for the Philadelphia Athletics in 1948. Blackburne is best known for the creation of baseball rubbing mud, used to remove the finish on new baseballs and give pitchers better grip and control. A newly manufactured baseball has a slick and glossy finish that needs to be reduced without damaging or discoloring it and a specially prepared mud is used to do that.

Before the discovery of rubbing mud, the slickness of a baseball was removed with a mixture of infield dirt and water, but the practice discolored the balls. Other substances were tried, like shoe polish, tobacco juice, and soil taken from beneath stadium bleachers. But they all scratched or damaged the ball's leather. The problem remained unsolved until the late 1930's.

That was when Blackburne, at the time a coach with Philadelphia, set out in search of a good "rubbing mud". He found it not far from his home, on the New Jersey side of the Delaware River. While he kept the exact location secret, he harvested the mud and after cleaning and screening it sold it to Major League Baseball as Lena Blackburne Baseball Rubbing Mud. Blackburne died in 1968 and left his business to a friend, who then passed it on to his sons, and today the company still contracts with MLB to sell the mud. Each year the company dispatches a crew to the mud's secret location to collect 1,000 pounds that is stored over the winter for the next season.

"If anybody happens to catch us in the act of harvesting the mud," the company owner said, "I come up with a story to give them a reason I'm putting mud in a bucket. I've told people I use it in my garden, I use it for my rose bushes, I use it for bee stings and poison ivy and any kind of story."

Before every game the game's supply of baseballs is rubbed with Blackburne's Mud, in accordance with MLB Rule 4.01(c),which states that all baseballs "shall be properly rubbed so that the gloss is removed."

The mud has been described as "very fine, like thick chocolate pudding."

6

Glove Story

"Don't let it happen again, or I'll have to tell your Dad."
—Groundskeeper, upon returning the author's
misplaced glove

This is a love story.

In 1958, the year I turned nine, my father took me to my first major
league game. The Senators were playing the Kansas City Athletics
in Washington's Griffith Stadium on a sunny Saturday afternoon.
We drove into the city, Dad parked the car in a small, crowded lot, and
we walked the last remaining blocks to the stadium, which was in a
busy neighborhood surrounded so closely by buildings and shops that it
was hidden from our view and not until we were approaching the gate
and Dad was taking the tickets from his pocket did I look up to see the
light towers and know we were there.

Inside the stadium the concourse was poorly lit and narrow with a
low ceiling. But when we climbed a ramp and emerged from the dark
underground to enter the lower grandstands, the ballfield fanned out
under a bright, sunlit sky. The outfield was the purest green, a color
Crayola should have marketed as *Ballpark Green*. It was beautiful. The
game hadn't begun and I was already spellbound.

It was the moment all fans experience: their first time, when they
take in a ballfield's glorious panorama without the confining edges of a
TV screen—in my case, a black-and-white one— and are mesmerized
by what they see. Impossibly, they try to take it all in at once. For
several moments that's what I did, not moving another step. The leftfield

bleachers seemed farther and the rightfield wall higher than I had imagined. The crown of a mammoth tree peeked over the top of the centerfield wall, reminding me that the wall held in the game while a real world still went on outside. Players were scattered everywhere playing catch or shagging flies, and the bowl of the double-decked stadium held a chorus of distinct sounds: the chants of vendors, the chatter of a gathering crowd, and the echo of the rifle shots of batting practice.

We sat in box seats down the line from first base. Dad bought a hot dog for me and a beer for himself. Russ Kemmerer pitched for the Senators—my team—and not well. When Hector Lopez hit a home run that barely reached the leftfield seats to give the A's a lead they would not relinquish, I was stunned with disbelief, even though I had seen the ball clear the fence. The home crowd was still. Kemmerer looked down and pawed at the dirt on the mound with his cleats. As he crossed first base, Lopez shifted into his home run trot, but I needed confirmation. Where was Bob Wolfe at the microphone to describe the play in his excited baritone voice? As Hector continued past second base, I looked up at Dad to see him shake his head sadly. So this was what a home run was like. Nobody announced it. You had to figure it out for yourself; when the ball disappears and the outfielder comes down against the wall with an empty glove, there is only one possibility. The Senators lost that day. They lost often in those days. They were perennially in last place.

I was not an avid reader as a kid but one of the first books that attracted me was the novel *The Year the Yankees Lost the Pennant*. It's the story of a diehard Senators fan—Joe Boyd—who trades his soul with the devil to become Joe Hardy, a baseball star who leads the Senators to the pennant over the Yankees, the team I hated at that age. I loved the book. I saw my baseball devotion in it. I would have traded places with Joe Boyd/Hardy in a heartbeat. Many years later I read a newer edition that included an introduction comparing Joe's compromising decision with the choice of modern players to use steroids. The devil is present in both situations.

Before Griffith Stadium was torn down four years later I watched some of the game's immortals play there, Ted Williams winning the

1958 batting title in a doubleheader on the last weekend of the season, and Mickey Mantle and Harmon Killebrew hitting home runs in 1959. I was in the grandstands when Roger Maris hit his 54th in 1961.

My hero back then was Roy Sievers, the Nats' best player and the American League home run champ in 1957. Roy was an all-star playing for a last place team before the days of free agency but did his best, soldiering on and standing tall like Gary Cooper facing difficult odds in the streets of *High Noon*. But Roy was traded to the White Sox for Earl Battey, who became the starting catcher for the team that would win the pennant six years later, but in another city when they weren't my team anymore. But that's another story.

The Sievers trade was my first lost love. But it was a move that helped the Senators finally become winners. With Chuck Stobbs and Rocky Bridges and a host of other everyday players from the last-place team replaced by future stars like Killebrew and Bob Allison and Zoilo Versalles, the Senators climbed out of the American League cellar in 1960 with a bright future ahead of them.

But on a dark November morning that year, with spring training and hope of a better season still three months away, Dad slid the *Washington Post* across the breakfast table toward me and I read the most despairing front page news: the Senators were moving to Minnesota.

The team's owner, Calvin Griffith, was committing high treason. How could he do this to me? How could he do this to the city? One man couldn't pick up Washington's beloved team and move it halfway across the country, even if he owned it. Washington without a baseball team—how could it be? For years afterwards, I turned my anger into a loathing of the Twins. Washington got a new team, an expansion franchise also named the Senators, to whom I swore an allegiance that was strong in the Chuck Hinton era but weakened when I went off to college. It was a good thing, too. If not, when the new Senators moved to Texas to become the Rangers, I may not have survived a second betrayal. Thus, Washington—the nation's capital—became the first city to lose two Major League teams.

All good love stories must include some heartache.

I switched my allegiance to another team in another league. This was not easy for an 11-year old to do. I became a Pittsburgh Pirate fan, in part because the small transistor radio I got as a birthday present was strong enough to pick up Pirate games at night amidst the static coming over the Allegheny Mountains. I would turn off my bedroom light and lay in the dark and finger the radio dial with a safecracker's precision until I found KDKA and heard Bob Prince in his unmistakable hillbilly drawl call Pirate games and the heroics of their star player, Roberto Clemente. I idolized Clemente like nobody since Sievers. In those days televised games were rare, and fans in American League cities like me never got to see National League games. But I only needed to see Clemente once in an All-Star Game to burn an image of him in my mind that would last the rest of the season. On many nights in my dark bedroom Bob Prince's announcement that Clemente was coming to bat was all I needed to create a mental picture of him clearer than any TV screen, digging in with his cleats and rolling his shoulders and twisting his neck and swinging off his front foot—just as I had seen him do in the All-Star game. I didn't need a TV. I saw Clemente play a hundred times. A love affair does that for you.

I played outfield on my high school team: the TC Williams Titans. I attended TC for two years and was in the school's first graduating class, an upperclassman both years. The first year, our senior-less team lost its first game in a no-hitter. We finished the year 4 and 13. We eked out a win against George Washington, the high school I had attended in 9th and 10th grades. We lost to Fort Hunt on a field without outfield fences, where, playing leftfield, I misplayed a line drive hit directly at me, taking my first step forward as the ball rocketed over my head. The ball skipped 350 feet to where the grass gave way to an endless slab of blacktop and continued to roll so far the batter could have run around the bases three or four times before I retrieved it. But I felt it was my duty—and my penance—to chase it no matter how far. It was a low point in a season of lows.

There was a high point a week later. We played Edison, always tough. I came to the plate with one out and Randy McCollum on third and from the 3rd base coaching box Coach gave me the bunt sign. What? I stared at him. He had to repeat the sign. Squeeze bunt? Yes. A suicide squeeze bunt. As an inside curve broke toward my knees, in the corner of my eye I saw Randy chugging toward me like a runaway train. My teammates told me later that I was holding the bat at a comically oblique angle, with its head pointed toward the ground, when it miraculously struck the arc of the pitch. In the blink of an eye I saw the ball rolling in the thick grass toward first base. I ran and passed it thirty feet from home plate. The pitcher overthrew first and I ended up on third. We won 3-2.

As a senior—my second and last season—I started strong. On opening day against Mount Vernon I had two hits, scored a run, knocked in another, and threw out a runner trying to score from second on a single. At practice the next day Coach singled me out. "Field, keeping playing like that and you're in the starting line-up every game."

It was going to be a great season.

Next, we faced crosstown rival Hammond and its southpaw hurler named Johnny Green, not a flame thrower, but a Bobby Shantz (*see New York Yankees, 1958 roster*), slight in build and in command of a nasty curve that could break hard. I was a left-hand batter, and when Green realized his big bender was a pitch I would never hit, curves were all I saw. I could have left my bat in the dugout and done no worse. The sight of the ball spinning at my head had me leaning back and ducking, and after I watched the first couple pitches break over the plate for strikes I began a survival strategy of flailing at pitches no matter where they were, like I was swatting insects. It must have been a pitiful sight. Oh-for-three, without even hitting a foul ball.

I was benched in our next game. And for several games after that. My saving grace was that I could hit righties while our other left fielder, Roger Snowden, also a senior, could not. He looked as pitiful facing righties as I did against lefties. Coach adopted Casey Stengel's (*again, Yankees, 1958*) platooning strategy of starting Roger against lefties and me against righties.

We played well enough to make the year-end playoffs. Our opponent in the first round would be top-ranked Edison. Edison had two ace hurlers. One threw left and the other right, and the question of whether Roger or I would start in our biggest game of the year wasn't answered until we got off the bus at Alexandria's Municipal Stadium and I peered over at the Edison bullpen and saw the right-hander warming up.

The game was close, well-played, and tense. Edison led 1-0 in the bottom of the 7th—the last inning. I led off and drew a walk. Given that it could be our last game—and the last game of Roger's high school career—Coach sent him in to run for me and then gave the next batter the signal to sacrifice bunt. He made contact, but not squarely, and launched the ball on a low rainbow arc toward the third baseman, who raced in and dove and rolled with the ball clutched in his glove, but the umpire's signal came late and it was unclear to Roger whether or not the ball had been caught in the air. He stood frozen in the basepath fifteen feet off first base waiting for the call. By the time the "out" signal was made, the third baseman was on his feet throwing to first to double up Roger. One out later the game—and our season—was over. For years I wondered if I would have reacted differently had I been on base in place of Roger and concluded that I was lucky to have been in the dugout at the time.

I probably saw a hundred Major League games in person and maybe a thousand on TV before experiencing two diamond gems the dreams of which had sustained me all those years: catching a foul ball at a game and witnessing in person the 7th game of a World Series. In a 1997 game Denny Hocking of the Twins fouled a pitch from Andy Pettitte of the Yankees that landed in my outstretched hands. I went home that night and placed it next to Charlie, 5 months old, sleeping in his crib. Six years earlier Anne and I had been at the Metrodome to see Games 6 and 7 of the '91 World Series. Kirby Puckett won the 6th game with a homer in the 11th inning, and then the next night Jack Morris pitched his complete-game masterpiece, winning a 10-inning shutout. The best 1-0 baseball game ever. Certainly better than TC Williams vs. Edison in 1967.

But in ways that mattered most, as I was entering my 50th year, the game was slipping away from me. I hadn't seen my glove for years. Nor had I gripped a bat or tossed a ball. It had never occurred to me that I might be missing something. Being a spectator to the game was enough, or so I thought. Then, without realizing it, I began a comeback.

In July that year along with two friends—Phil and Jim—I visited the baseball diamond that had been cut from an Iowa cornfield for the movie *Field of Dreams*. Because of the movie's success the field was left as a tourist attraction, and visitors made pilgrimages there to walk across the outfield or along the edge of the corn stalks in solemn silence like it was some sort of sacred shrine. Dads took turns in front of the mound pitching underhanded to their sons at home plate. The three of us had brought gloves and a ball and bat and we claimed some space for ourselves in left field—Shoeless Joe's position—to shag flies. I watched Phil swing and launch a fly ball and looked up to track its arc against an Iowa blue sky. Overcome by memories, I suddenly remembered something about my love of baseball I had forgotten, that in high school I had enjoyed practices as much as games, a peculiar affection for sure. It was baseball's mechanics I loved the most, the simple acts of swinging a bat and throwing and catching, not the keeping score or winning or losing. Just *playing* was enough. All this came back to me as I camped under Phil's flyball on the Field of Dreams. When it was my turn to hit, after adjusting for several misses, I tossed the ball up and swung and sent it skyward to the reassuring sound of a wood bat striking a ball. I had rediscovered an old friend.

The following year, when Charlie started playing little league, I volunteered to coach. For my comeback I treated myself by purchasing a new glove, my first new glove since high school. I went all out. I wasn't a kid this time around. I had a good job with a good salary, so I bought a classic, a Rawlings Heart-Of-The Hide, real leather, a pitcher's glove with a small, perfect pocket that could curl around a ball and squeeze it all by itself.

I went on to coach for six years.

After one of Charlie's games I drove home mistakenly thinking the glove, which by now was broken in and flexed perfectly and felt as natural on my right hand as skin, was in Charlie's bat bag, but I discovered it was missing and drove back to the ball field to look for it in the dark with a flashlight. I searched for an hour, looking everywhere. But it wasn't there. I returned home as sad as I could remember. I was crushed. It felt like I had lost my best dog; the glove that was part of me was gone.

On my way to work in the morning I drove by the field again, where I asked a groundskeeper if he had found a lost glove. Southpaw? Yes. He went into his shop and came out a moment later with my glove. I was the happiest guy in the world when he handed it to me, saying, "Don't let it happen again, or I'll have to tell your Dad."

A good love story includes a journey, a return to a place to find something that had been lost. This story ends where it began: on a ballfield. In the last chapter of my baseball life I found a joy greater than I ever knew watching Charlie play and grow with the game. I cheered when he succeeded and grieved when he failed. The highs and lows were greatly magnified compared to my playing days. If he struck out in a game with runners in position to score, I felt a pain greater than what Johnny Green's wicked curve had inflicted on me forty years ago. But when he delivered a game-winning hit and his teammates rushed onto the field to greet him, I was delirious with an elation that could wash away the feeling of how crumby my day may have been up to that point.

Over the years I don't know how many pitches I threw to him in batting cages. Five thousand. Six thousand. The bucket held forty or fifty balls. In each session we seldom went through less than three buckets. Fifteen or twenty sessions in a season. I did it for him, and for me. I told him once that I would never say no if it was his idea. And we played catch, just as my father had done with me in the side yard when I was Charlie's age. Back then my Dad wore the pancake first baseman's mitt of his generation. My Rawlings Heart-of-the-Hide snapped when Charlie burned one into the middle of the pocket. It made a heavenly sound. I told my wife I want to be buried with that glove on my hand someday.

The game is meant for fathers and sons. It creates opportunities for lessons. In a game once Charlie was playing third base when a runner slid under his tag. But the umpire called him out and the coach of the other team, who saw the play clearly from less than ten feet away, argued fiercely. For a moment he was on a collision course with ejection. He and the ump would have been bumping chests if Charlie—half their heights—had not been standing in between them like a pawn stuck between two bishops on a chessboard. The sheepish expression on his face told me he had a secret, that he knew the runner to be safe. I had taught him about truth and honesty and he was clearly conflicted. But the incident passed and the game went on. In the car on the way home he confessed. I told him I knew the runner was safe. He wanted to know how he should have answered if the other team's coach had asked him *safe or out*?

This was to be a great teaching moment for me. Life is not always black and white. The truth can be lost. But not in baseball. There is no ambiguity in baseball.

"First of all," I said, "I wouldn't allow it. I would have run onto the field and scolded the other coach for asking you directly. Only *I* am allowed to speak to my players".

"But," I continued, "if you really wanted to say something, there's a right answer in baseball that is never a lie, but part of baseball's own justice system."

"Charlie," I replied, "you could have said, 'The ump called him out'. It would have been the truth."

That's my love story, my glove story.

7

The Arms Race

"Stand behind a tree 60 feet away and I'll whomp you with an optical illusion."
— Hall-Of-Fame pitcher Dizzy Dean, when told a curve ball was just an optical illusion.

Baseball is a team game in which players must perform on their own. They are strictly solo acts—batting or fielding—and are expected to do both well. To borrow a football expression, baseball players must play *both sides of the ball*.

Except for the pitcher and designated hitter, baseball has no specialists like in football, where a punt returner or a long snapper or a pass rusher for third-and-long situations comes in for one play and then sits down again. Baseball's only brush with specialization is the lefty/ righty thing of pitchers and batters.

The duel between pitcher and batter is unique in all of sports. It's a marvelous thing to watch, the greatest showdown of two athletes on which a team game's outcome depends. It's *mano-a-mano*, with little help coming from teammates. There are no assists, traps, blocks, double-teams, or screens, and neither gets to sit out a play just because they need a blow. When somebody pinch-hits for them, they're gone from the game, not to return.

"What is life after all, but a challenge," Hall-Of-Fame pitcher Warren Spahn once said. "And what better challenge can there be than the one between the pitcher and hitter?" Then, he added, "Hitting is timing. Pitching is upsetting timing."

Hitting a baseball well is hard. This can be seen by measuring the elements involved in hitting. Start with the strike zone, which is approximately 17 inches wide and two feet tall. That means a hitter must defend a zone that is 400 square inches. A little known fact is that the actual strike zone is not a plane, but is a volume of 4½ cubic feet extending from the front to the back of home plate. Any pitch passing through the volume can be called a strike.

The thickest part of a bat is only 2¼ inches wide. To strike a ball solidly, a batter must hit a pitch with its center about 6 inches from the end. That reduces the critical contact area between bat and ball to approximately two square inches. A Major League fastball reaches the plate in less than half a second on a path that is never straight, and in that time a batter must detect its speed, spin, and location, decide whether or not to swing, and swing through the strike zone at 70 miles per hour to have even the remotest chance of hitting the ball. I once read something a hitting expert said, that it is more likely for a pitcher to accidentally throw a pitch in the way of a hitter's swing than for the hitter to make good contact on his own.

A good pitcher needs an arsenal of pitches. If all he threw were straight fastballs, regardless of their speed, a Major League batter could probably hit them all. A former pitcher once said, "When a Major League hitter gets what he's looking for and knows it's coming, it's all aboard for a ride to the moon."

Good pitching is an art of deception.

Pitchers start to develop *good stuff* in high school. I go to high school games and will stand behind the backstop to view the battle between pitchers and batters and up close the contest looks no different than in the Majors. The exception is high school players don't get an unlimited supply of clean, white baseballs and by the late innings pitchers are throwing recycled balls that are scuffed and gray. Still, high school teams take the arms race seriously. At one game I noticed the catcher was wearing an earpiece to receive pitch instructions from the dugout instead of hand signals.

Of course, with few exceptions even the best 17-year-old pitchers don't have Major League speed. They make up for it by mixing pitches and varying their break and location. Many pitches don't do what they're supposed to, but then few high schoolers hit like Joe Mauer did at that age and so pitchers will get away with mistakes. But throw a mistake to a good hitter? A pitch that just hangs high in the strike zone? It's like setting the ball on a tee for the batter. Just as in the Majors, good hitters hammer mistakes deep into outfield gaps.

Good location is a pitcher's best weapon at any level, and it's critical when he's pitching to a dangerous hitter. At the Cooperstown Hall-Of-Fame there is a model of Ted Williams's strike zone that illustrates the point. The model depicts his strike zone with a rectangular array of 77 baseballs, each painted with a different batting average, what Ted felt his average was when he swung at pitches in that location. Two balls only two inches apart are painted .400 and .230, with the higher average closer to the heart of the zone. A pitcher missing by only two inches with Ted would get a ride to the moon.

"Home plate is seventeen inches wide," Warren Spahn said. "but I ignore the middle twelve inches. I pitch to the two-and-a-half inches on each side."

Hall-Of-Famer Greg Maddux's location was legendary. With only one outstanding pitch—a two-seamed fastball he perfected after giving up on the faster four seamer—he won 350 games as a "control" pitcher, i.e., one known for great location. Two seamers move more than four-seamers, and even if Maddux didn't get a lot of speed from his, it moved well enough while staying inside the strike zone to give batters fits. He was famous for filling up a strike zone and not wasting pitches. After the pitch count was added to all the other stats kept in a baseball game, a sportswriter coined the term "a Maddux" to denote a game in which the winning pitcher went a full nine innings on less than a hundred pitches. Maddux himself holds the record. He threw 13 Madduxes.

Pitch counts are watched more closely nowadays. When a pitcher nears 100, his bullpen starts to stir. Compare this with the game's past. In 1963 the Milwaukee Braves and San Francisco Giants played a 16-inning game in which both pitchers—Spahn and Juan Marichal—went the distance, each throwing more than 200. The Giants won 1-0 on a homerun by Willie Mays. Spahn said the screwball he threw to Mays was the biggest mistake of his legendary career.

Pitchers throw a greater variety of pitches today compared to when the game was invented and thus are much tougher to hit. But hitters have gotten better, too. Still, we've probably seen the last four-hundred hitter (Williams, in 1941) and the last 30-game winner (Denny McClain, in 1968).

In its original version baseball was strictly a hitter's game. It was *meant* to be a hitter's game. Pitchers were instructed to throw underhand and not deceive hitters. This created high-scoring games lasting for hours. But changes were inevitable. The first one allowed pitchers to get a running start like in a cricket match. Next came throwing overhand. When batters still weren't getting fooled, pitchers began smearing mud or spitting on the ball to gain an advantage.

While throwing underhand, a pitcher was required to move his arm like a pendulum, straight and swinging perpendicular at his side, to prevent spinning and sideways motion to his pitches. Then, one day a pitcher named Candy Cummings, remembering how he had been able to get clamshells to curve when he tossed them at the beach as a boy, experimented with a pitch in which he twisted and snapped his wrist—a pitching motion that had been banned by the rules of the Players Association—and in doing so invented the curveball. Eventually, the rules were relaxed and all pitchers began to perfect their curves.

The curveball was like an ultimate weapon, the first new pitch invented to give pitchers an advantage in the arms race. There would be more to come.

There is an interesting story about the history of the curveball, that for the longest time few people actually believed it curved. In the 1930's, even though its sideways motion was hard to miss, a curveball was thought to be an optical illusion, Dizzy Dean, a great pitcher of that era, answered the deniers. "Stand behind a tree 60 feet away and I'll whomp you with an optical illusion." Then, in 1959 the National Institute for Standards and Technology conducted tests and studies to prove *curveballs really curved* by using physics, not by beaning batters. The *New York Times* ran an article of the Institute's findings under the headline *U.S. Upholds Curve.* The article explained how air whirlpools around a thrown baseball and causes the pressure on one side to be greater than on the other. It was 1959, and the story diverted the attention of *Times* readers away from serious news about the Cold War, nuclear tests, and a revolution in Cuba.

I own a book called *The Physics Of Baseball*, written by a Yale professor who uses equations and illustrations to explain why a curveball breaks or why a fastball can't rise. In a series of math equations he estimates how far a ball can actually be hit. I'm convinced that if I had that book in high school, my physics grade would have been a lot better.

The knuckleball is the preferred pitch of aging pitchers whose arm strength isn't what it used to be. Thrown with zero spin, passing air grabs a baseball's stitches randomly to give it unpredictable movement on its path to the plate. Batters don't know what the ball will do. Neither do catchers. Gus Triandoes of the Baltimore Orioles used an oversized mitt in the 1960's when catching the famous knuckleballer Hoyt Wilhelm.

Baseball's best hitters have seemingly been unaffected by pitchers' gains in the arms race. Hank Aaron, one of the game's greatest sluggers, never thought pitchers held much of an advantage. "The pitcher has only a ball," he said. "I've got a bat. So, the percentage of weapons is in my favor and I let the fellow with the ball do the fretting."

A slider thrown well is a nasty pitch to hit. It's like a curveball at high speed. If thrown with the same delivery as a fastball, hitters have no idea it will break until it's too late. Its invention has given some pitchers a decided edge in the arms race.

In his prime the Dodger's Sandy Koufax was baseball's most dominant pitcher. He threw only fastballs and curves but threw them both so well batters couldn't hit either, even if they knew which pitch was coming. But Sandy felt he should try another pitch and one day began to develop a slider. He practiced it on the sidelines and when he felt he was ready chose an upcoming game against the Milwaukee Braves—and Hank Aaron—to try it out. He figured if he could get Aaron out with his slider, he could get anybody out.

The Dodgers were playing the Braves in Milwaukee's County Stadium. When Aaron came to bat, Koufax threw him a slider. Aaron hit it over the fence, but foul by a few feet. He turned to catcher John Roseboro and asked, "What was that pitch?"

Roseboro said it was a slider.

Aaron replied, "Tell Sandy he doesn't need that pitch."

Fifty years later the Dodgers had a pitcher whose slider was deadly. Clayton Kershaw threw his with movement that defied physics. From a seat behind home plate once I watched him pitch against the Twins on a chilly day in early April. Kershaw's sliders were breaking and dropping two feet and, combined with a unique delivery that prevented hitters from picking up his release point, had Twins waving their bats like they were swatting flies. He fanned thirteen, and when I say *fanned*, I mean the Twins, thinking that fastballs were coming at them, were swinging at *air*. Kershaw was throwing sliders that disappeared on them.

I still have the scorecard I kept for the game and it shows Kershaw retiring Twins hitters one-two-three with one or two strikeouts every inning. The Twins had only three batted balls that left the infield. I couldn't recall ever attending a game in which a pitcher was so dominant.

Kershaw didn't allow a single baserunner through seven innings. For seven innings, he was perfect, twenty-one batters up, twenty-one batters down. I trembled thinking I might be witnessing a baseball rarity, a *perfect game*. In the context of baseball's arm race, perfect is the right word, as I realized luck and hitters' mistakes have something to do with it, but in a perfect game the pitcher is *perfect*.

The Twins crowd was cheering for Kershaw as he left the mound after the 7th inning. So was I, but I was also peering into the Dodger's dugout where I saw manager Dave Roberts place an arm on Kershaw's shoulder and speak to him softly. When Kershaw nodded, and was mobbed by teammates after the conversation ended, I knew what Roberts had said to him, that perfect or not, Kershaw had to come out of the game. A lockout that spring had shortened spring training and the year before the Dodgers had exited the National League playoffs early in part because they lost Kershaw to arm trouble. So, the Dodgers were balancing their desire to beat the Twins with the need to protect the condition of their best pitcher on a chilly day in April.

The crowd booed when they saw Dodger reliever Alex Vesia trot in from the bullpen at the start of the 8th.

"There's a point where I've got to decide," Roberts told the press after the game, "'To what end?' I'm as big a fan as anyone, and I'm a fan of Clayton and to see a battery of him and Austin (his catcher) throw a perfect game or a no-hitter, I'm all in. But, again, to what end? To what cost?" Then, he added, "There's a lot of people cheering for the Dodgers, not only just for this game and for Clayton to throw a no-hitter, but for the Dodgers to win the World Series. For us to do that, we need him healthy."

The Dodgers won 7-0. After retiring the first batter in the 8th on a groundout, Vesia gave up a single to catcher Gary Sanchez, the Twin's first hit, and first base runner, too. He walked Max Kepler but escaped the inning without further damage. In the 9th he put the Twins down 1-2-3 to preserve the combined one-hit shutout.

Kershaw had thrown only 80 pitches. Not only did he have a chance for a perfect game, he had a chance for a Maddux, too. But he won the game, his first win in a season in which he would give the Dodgers 126 innings and win 12 games.

To the list of pitches used to win the arms race, add something else: intimidation. A pitch thrown to knock a batter down.

Bob Gibson of the St. Louis Cardinals was famous for intimidation. Besides being a fierce, unrelenting competitor with a determination seldom seen in a pitcher, Gibson threw "chin music", pitches high and tight not necessarily to hit a batter, but to make him think he'll be hit. It sent the message *don't dig in against me.* Bill White, a Cardinal teammate and close friend of Gibson's, was traded to Philadelphia and knew exactly what would happen the first time they faced each other, that Gibson would throw at him. And that's what happened. When Gibson put White on the ground in the batter's box, he was saying *we're not teammates anymore.*

The Cardinals met the Detroit Tigers in the 1968 World Series after a year in which Gibson had won the National League arms race like nobody since Christy Mathewson. Consider these numbers: 34 starts with 28 complete games, 13 shutouts, a 22-9 record, and an astoundingly low E.R.A. of 1.12. In addition to a great slider, his pitch arsenal consisted of fastball, changeup, curve, and knockdown.

In Game 1 of the Series Gibson was nearly unhittable. In front of a home crowd of 55,000 Cardinal fans he went to the mound to start the 9th inning with a 4-0 lead. Mickey Stanley singled for the Tigers, only their 5th hit of the game. The next batter, the dangerous Al Kaline, struck out on a Gibson fastball. The crowd roared.

A moment later there was another roar, louder this time. The Cardinal catcher, Tim McCarver, straightening to toss the ball back to Gibson, hesitated, and Gibson, notorious for being swift on the mound, glowered at him while motioning for the ball. McCarver pointed with his gloved hand at something behind Gibson's head.

Gibson, still staring at his catcher, yelled, "Throw the goddam ball back, will you! C'mon, let's go!"

Continuing to hold the ball, McCarver pointed again, and this time Gibson turned around to read a message on the center-field scoreboard that until that moment everyone in the ballpark except him had seen. *Gibson's 15th strikeout ties the all-time World Series record held by Sandy Koufax.*

Still surrounded by deafening crowd noise, Gibson dug at the mound dirt with his spikes and then doffed his cap. "I *hate* that sort of thing," he said later.

He proceed to strike out the next batter, Norm Cash, with a slider. There were two outs. Willie Horton was next. With a two-and-two count, McCarver called for a slider and Gibson threw a pitch that seemed to be heading toward Horton's rib cage. Horton flinched and pulled back rapidly, but the pitch broke suddenly away from him and caught the inside edge of the plate for strike three and the game was over. Seventeen strike outs. A World Series record, and still is, most likely never to be topped.

Years later, McCarver said about the game, "I can still see that last pitch, and I'll bet Willie Horton thinks to this day that the ball hit him. That's how much it broke. Talk about a batter shuddering."

Football has nothing to compare to baseball's arms race, but I'll concede that quarterbacks are just as important to their teams as baseball pitchers are to theirs. Football has its Kershaws and Gibsons. They must offer a variety of passes to fool their opponents. And they do. They throw short passes and long passes.

8

Townball

This is the heart of my thesis, that in addition to being a perfect game, baseball can give us things we seem to have lost and wish to reclaim: a timeless treasure, a sense of community, and a shared common purpose. We may search for these things in a number of places but my thesis is they are found in baseball games played in pastoral settings like the one we imagine in baseball's creation story if it had been real.

It's called townball. It's amateur baseball played in thousands of small towns across the country—mostly in the Midwest—by men of all ages with day jobs, careers, and lives outside of the game but who devote their summer evenings and weekends to playing baseball for their neighbors and friends without getting paid. For amateurs, they play a pretty good game, one that looks highly professional. For some, the best players, townball may be a temporary stopover on their way up to playing professionally—whether in a high minor league or perhaps the Major Leagues—and for some it is a stop on their way back down.

Most town ballers started playing after high school or in the off seasons of their college teams. Many are still playing past age forty. They can't seem to give it up. After playing a game alongside teammates half their age, they will limp back to their cars clutching sore arms or shoulders. The younger players go to their cars with arms around girlfriends. Young or old, both are likely to meet at a bar in town.

Townball has been around a long time. It's over a hundred years old. Minnesota has three hundred townball teams, the most of any state. Towns are proud to have their own teams and keep stories about their history and greatest players. They play on ballfields set in landscapes resembling a scene from a W.P. Kinsella short story or a Norman Rockwell painting.

Picture yourself as a traveler searching for that landscape.

It's Sunday afternoon.

You're driving through farm country when you enter a town with a welcome sign that says Miesville or Cornbelt or Prairie View. As you slow down, you take in familiar sights. There's a gas station and a feed store. A church with a well-kept lawn and cemetery. The main street is off to the side of the highway. A bar and grill advertises a Friday night fish fry. You pass a park with a picnic shelter and a bandstand, and a memorial honoring the town's war veterans. As you admire the town's pleasant tidiness and order, a ballfield catches your eye. It has lights and a covered set of bleachers and a scoreboard advertising a local business. And a sign announcing a game that day. There are no traffic lights in the town to stop you and after the ballfield you're suddenly back out in the country again.

You turn around and go back.

You park your car in a grass meadow beyond the field's outfield fence and buy a ticket for three dollars in a booth behind home plate. A sign says it's to help pay for players' uniforms. You take a seat in the bleachers, which are several rows deep and behind a screen hung between the dugouts. An overhead roof shades you from the afternoon sun. The bleachers fill up with town's people who seem to know each other.

When you look out through the screen at the ballfield you are pleased with what you see. The infield is perfectly shaped and trimmed with a lawn of thick green grass. The baselines are brightly chalked. Beyond the infield dirt the green lawn continues to the outfield fence, and you think you didn't expect the field to be so well groomed and cared for, not for an amateur game. It's beautiful by itself, even without the game having begun.

Down one foul line a coach with a fungo bat lofts flyballs to players clustered in the outfield. Another hits grounders to players at their infield positions, while a catcher without his gear on stands to his side taking return throws. The starting pitchers are warming up in foul territory. It's typical pre-game and all so familiar. When the players are ready and have returned to their dugouts, a member of the grounds crew carefully chalks the batters' boxes at home plate, just like at Target Field before a Twins game, except this guy does it alone.

The coaches meet at home plate to exchange lineups and go over ground rules with two umpires. You stand with your hand over your heart for the National Anthem, sung acapella by a woman introduced as the choir director of a local church. When the starting lineups are introduced it's by an announcer seated behind you in a raised crow's nest. For the home team, he adds flourish to his voice as players sprint from the dugout to their positions on the field when their names are announced. He declares "Play Ball," and the visiting team's leadoff hitter knocks the weight off the bat he's been swinging and strolls to the plate. He says something to the catcher and they smile to each other. He smooths the dirt under him with his cleats. The game begins.

It's good baseball. It's polished, well played, and competitive. The players never ease up. The pitcher's speed isn't recorded on the outfield scoreboard but you can still tell he's throwing hard, and from your seat behind home plate you see how his pitches move and drop to corners of the strike zone. Batters look for strikes to hit and run hard on grounders that infielders pull smoothly to their chests. Outfielders have strong arms. You applaud when the right fielder throws a frozen rope on one hop to the plate that cuts down a runner trying to score from second on a single.

Other things catch your attention. You guess the crowd to be several hundred and remember the town's population stated on the city limit sign was about the same. Some in attendance are seated down the foul lines past the dugouts in lawn chairs they brought with them. Many stand in groups around picnic tables behind the dugouts, shouting out the names of players after they make good plays. At the start of every inning the announcer reminds youngsters in the crowd they're paid a dollar for every foul ball they chase down and return. Several kids with gloves pace excitedly. In some innings, the reward amount is increased.

The players wear batting gloves but don't step out of the batter's box after each pitch to adjust them. They don't even step from the box.

When the pitcher gets the ball back from the catcher, he's ready to throw again. Bats are wood and make a solid reassuring sound when a ball is hit sharply. The players have to pick up their own bats on their way back to the dugout.

The fans talk amongst themselves. You try to pick out the wives or girlfriends of certain players. When they call out a player by name, the player smiles, but only for a second. His steely expression returns at once. His mind is on the game. Plays made with major league skill are rewarded with hearty applause and shouts of appreciation. The shortstop boots a groundball and then on the very next play atones himself turning a double play with elegance worthy of an ESPN highlight film. Fans cheer for both teams and you think that many of them came to see the visiting team.

The outfield wall is covered with the colorful ads of local businesses. They're hard to see amidst all the ad text but the distances to left, center, and right field are on the wall, too. There's a single concession stand behind the home team dugout where a line of customers never lets up. Next to it is a small shop selling team merchandise. Prices—food and merchandise— are just a fraction of what they are at Target Field.

It's a warm day under a high blue sky. Beyond the outfield wall a planted field rolls and swells in the sunshine all the way to the horizon. Rows of corn are sprouting up. You feel a breeze blowing in and notice how it raises the flag on the pole in the left field corner.

The home team is winning. Nobody is leaving early.

By the late innings you've drawn some conclusions about the game you're watching. You don't know the players but they show a devotion to their craft that matches Major Leaguers you've seen. Their game is not lacking in any of the abilities seen at a Major League game. Their game is the *same*. Another thought surprises you, that townball is enhanced by its surroundings. Everything goes together. The farm field beyond the fence. The simple compactness of the stadium, possessing everything the game demands of it. The ads on the outfield fence. The crowd alternating in its Sunday afternoon leisure and attentive enthusiasm for what's happening on the field. These observations make you feel certain you would see the *same* game watching townball anywhere, whether it's the Cold Spring Springers or the Miesville Mudhens, the Arlington A's or the Hibbing Miners.

But something else, too. It's *better* than what you're used to seeing. It's better because there are fewer distractions. They don't pull on your attention like at a Major League game. You aren't constantly being disturbed by a stadium announcer or scoreboard telling you to *look here* or *do this*. You aren't deafened by blaring music between innings. You get to appreciate the game *up close*. If there is a silly, between-inning game for fans to play, at least it's not some virtual aberration on the scoreboard. If it's a tire race, it's with a *real* tire and real people.

In the absence of high-decibel noise you have been able to hear the sounds of the game. The deep thump of a fastball when it strikes the catcher's glove. The sharp crack of a bat when a line drive is hit. The chatter from the dugouts and the umpire's bark when calling a strike. Hearing these sounds gives the game an intimacy. You can't hear these sounds in a Major League stadium.

In *Take Time For Paradise,* the late A. Bartlett Giamatti, who at one time served as Major League Baseball Commissioner, wrote that our culture is defined by what we do for leisure. He said shared leisure is good for a community. But he worried about where our leisure was headed. "It is going private," he wrote. "Potentially communal and civic, it is now simply private, to be neither shared or explained." He blamed it on technology, an excess of choices competing for our leisure, and an aversion to community. His book was written in 1989, the same year he died, and had he lived he might admit that shared leisure had been saved in townball. He would have liked what he saw there. The closeness of the game to the fans. The fan's closeness to the players as young men they know and share their community with. Their mutual respect for the game, and time spent together honoring that respect. Giamatti would have called it good shared leisure.

It's hard to worship the Major League game and its players today. The Majors have too many disruptions, certainly a lot more than when hero worshipping was easy, like when a 9-year-old boy idolized Roy Sievers. Our loyalty to the game is constantly tested by things that disturb us: player salaries, contract disputes, and free agency. Analytics that instruct batters to go deep into pitch counts and take too many strikes. Strikeouts that outnumber hits. Games that last too long. Pitch clocks. Umpires' calls that are challenged and too many pitching changes.

There is a difference between loving the game and loving those who play it. Understandably, fans want to get close to players. But they also want to know that players share their respect for the game. Fans retain illusions of the game being as it once was, before PED's and cheating scandals tainted it. Because of these and other dishonors, Major League players feel better off if fans don't really get to know them. They don't want to be idolized and fans accept this instinct. But a tension exists. When fans discover players are imperfect humans just like them and don't honor the game as they do, illusions of the players are shattered. And of the game, too, perhaps.

Townball keeps both illusions alive—for the game and for the players. Fans watch baseball played in all its traditional simplicity and pastoral beauty. Without analytics telling them what to do, players who aren't getting paid to play swing at good pitches and put the ball in play and fielders get to show their graceful skills. Teams bunt, steal, and hit and run, and coaches let their starting pitchers go deep into games. Amateur players play as hard as professionals without free agency hovering above them. We respect them even if we don't know their names or where they came from because we see how well and hard they play. There are no illusions of them as perfect human beings, just illusions of them as good ballplayers dedicated to playing an honorable game.

Some fans believe baseball's evolution and creation stories can co-exist without contradictions. If they would watch a townball game, they might say they're witnessing the same idyllic setting, leisurely rhythm, and timelessness of the creation story, that the evolution and creation stories meet there.

"Baseball's time is seamless and invisible," the great baseball author Roger Angel once wrote, "a bubble within which players move at exactly the same pace and rhythms as all their predecessors. This is the way the game was played in our youth and in our fathers' youth, and even back then—back in the country days—there must have been the same feeling that time could be stopped."

9

Infinity And The
Greatest Comeback

"*It ain't over 'til it's over.*"

Everybody—not just baseball fans—knows who said this. Yogi Berra. Yogi also said "90% of the game is half mental," and "If the people don't want to come out to the ballpark, nobody's gonna stop 'em." And when asked about a certain restaurant, he reportedly replied, "Nobody goes there anymore. It's too crowded."

We shouldn't try to overanalyze Yogi. We should just accept his remarks for what they are: truths expressed in a different language. There has never been a player in any sport like Yogi Berra, at the same time both an all-star athlete and an author of the most baffling remarks about his sport and life. He is a unique baseball treasure. *"It ain't over 'til it's over,"* is his most famous line and can be found in *Bartlett's Familiar Quotations* along with some of his other bewildering, yet truthful, remarks.

Baseball is the only game played without a clock and in theory a game could last forever. No lead is so great that the winning team can't blow it and lose the game. It *ain't over* until the final out is made. Time is infinite, and a baseball game can be, too. This isn't true in football or basketball, where time can run short and a game can be over before it *ain't over*. If the game clock is in a team's favor, a humungous lead can make losing impossible.

Not so in baseball.

A game was played in 2001 proved it.

Two of the best teams in the American League that year were the Cleveland Indians and the Seattle Mariners. By August the Indians were

60-48 and the Mariners were an astonishing 80-30. The Mariners would go on to finish the season 116-56. The two teams met in Cleveland in early August for a 3-game series, with Cleveland winning only one of the games. But how they won it made sports history and confirmed the wisdom of Yogi Berra.

By the 3rd inning the Mariners led 12-0 and Cleveland fans had given up. When their Indians put a tiny chip in the lead by scoring two runs in the 4th, the Mariners answered with two of their own to make the score 14-2, still a 12-run lead.

The 12-run lead continued into the 7th inning. Cleveland had only 9 outs to go, so to win they would need to score more runs than the number of outs they had left. I'm not sure what the football equivalent for this daunting task would be. I'll just say if there is one, no team has ever done it. Score five touchdowns in the 4th quarter? It has never happened.

Cleveland made their inevitable loss more respectable when they scored 3 runs in the 7th and another 4 in the 8th. When the 9th inning began, they still trailed by 5 runs. That they would lose seemed certain when two hitters made outs and batter Wil Cordero was down to his last strike with two runners on base. Cordero managed to walk to load the bases. The Indians were showing some life. They scored twice to cut the lead to 14-11.

The home crowd of Indian fans—those who hadn't left—came to the edges of their seats.

The bases were still loaded when Omar Visquel, their star shortstop, came to the plate. The count went to 3-2, which meant Indian baserunners would be going with the pitch, including James Lofton leading off first base. Visquel barely managed to keep the game going by fouling off the next two pitches. The Indians—and Visquel—were hanging on by the thinnest margin. Cleveland fans had to be thinking that after scoring nine unanswered runs their team had run out of miracles.

Seattle's first baseman was Ed Sprague, who earlier in the game had replaced John Olerud, the team's regular first baseman and itinerant all-star. In this situation, when the other team's potential winning run is at bat, conventional wisdom is to play a "no doubles" defense and guard the foul lines of an extra-base hit. But Sprague left too much space between himself and the rightfield line and when Visquel hit a hard grounder over first base it skipped under Sprague's outstretched glove as he dove to his left. The ball rolled all the way to the rightfield corner. Indian fans were on their feet hollering deliriously as they watched runners wheel around the bases. One scored, then another. Then, Lofton slid into home to tie the game at 14-14. Viszquel ended up on third with a triple.

It had been an astounding comeback.

The Indians stranded Viszquel with their third out. After scoring 12 runs with 8 outs, they finally used their last one. The game went into extra innings.

In the 11th Lofton was on second with one out when Jolbert Cabrera singled to shallow left field. Lofton was given the green light to go for home. The throw from the Mariners' leftfielder Mark McLemore was perfect, a strike on the fly into the catcher's waiting glove, but Lofton slid around the catcher's tag to score the winning run in the most amazing comeback in baseball history.

Only in a baseball game could a comeback from so far behind have taken place. It speaks to a wonderfully democratic aspect of the game, that teams are given an equal number of outs and outs aren't taken away just because a game appears to have been decided and time has run short.

"You can't sit on a lead and run a few plays into the line and just kill the clock," Earl Weaver said. "You've got to throw the ball over the plate and give the other man his chance. That's why baseball is the greatest game of them all."

Earl had just lost the World Series when he said those words and was entitled to some private grief, but he rose up in wisdom to acknowledge something special about his game. If a team can avoid using its last out, a game will go on forever, no matter what the other team does or wants to happen. It's wonderfully unique in baseball.

Baseball can't be bound by any dimension, not just time. All its dimensions are infinite, including physical ones. Take the foul poles. They don't just apply to the inside of a stadium. Their delineation of fair versus foul extends beyond the outfield walls, outside the ballpark, and over the distant horizon. They apply to a flyball traveling forever if it could be hit that far. The foul lines extend to infinity. Fair territory is an infinite domain, fanning out in endless width.

The infinite domain of fair territory applies to ballfields everywhere, large and small and arranged in all sorts of orientations. The fair territory of one covers the foul territory of another. Fair territories intersect and lay on to top of each other like blankets. That means there is no foul territory anywhere, and that *baseball's* fair territory covers the entire nation.

That's why baseball is the National Pastime.

10

Mona Lisa

My father told me something on my 12th birthday I never forgot. He said twelve was a tough age for a boy. "Twelve is too young for girls," he said, "and too old for baseball cards." He was wrong. If I could speak to him today, I would say, "Dad, you're *never* too old for baseball cards. And I think I've proven it."

I began collecting cards when I was nine. And I still am.

The first cards I bought were in 1958 in the middle of what some consider to be baseball's golden age, before expansion diluted the talent in the Major Leagues. 1958 cards were beautiful. They were cleanly designed and simple, with a cutout photo of the player set against a brightly colored background. I treasured them, not for their value as collector items, but for sentimental reasons. I worshipped the players.

I collected only Topps cards—and still do—which back then could be purchased in any corner drug store or supermarket. Topps reigned supreme in the baseball card market. As a 9-year-old, I didn't think of the cards as a business product, or something Topps made for profit, but rather as sort of a national treasure. I couldn't imagine being 9 years old without baseball cards. I would spend all my allowance money in the summer on them, and so did many of my friends.

The Topps story began in 1951.

In the fall of that year, just weeks after Bobby Thompson hit the shot heard 'round the world, his walk-off home run that won the pennant for the New York Giants, two men were sitting at a kitchen table in a small apartment in Brooklyn when they came up with the idea for a new product to sell: Major League baseball cards. They weren't trying to create works of art. They were just trying to produce a set of cards that would encourage kids to buy more bubble gum. Sy Berger was an intern with the Topps Chewing Gum Company and his friend Woody Gelman was a cartoonist and animator.

Topps had started as the American Tobacco Leaf Company but in the 1930's shifted to making gum, which had become a novelty product. Then, another gum company—Fleer Chewing Gum—changed the formula of its product to be less sticky and stretch better, a gum they marketed as bubble gum under the trade name Dubble Bubble.

After World War II Topps began making bubble gum, too, calling theirs Bazooka Gum, and as a market differentiator wrapped their pink gum bricks in comic strips that featured a character named Bazooka Joe. Four years later, under the Topps brand, the company packaged their gum with Hopalong Cassidy trading cards, Hopalong being a popular TV cowboy at the time played by an actor named William Boyd.

But on that day in his Brooklyn kitchen Berger told Gelman to design baseball cards that would be placed inside Topps gum packages. "It wasn't supposed to be about the cards," Berger said. "Topps was in the business of selling gum and we thought if they put a bunch of cards in a package with a stick of gum, it would boost sales." Gelman's idea was to put a photo of the player with his team and position on the front of the card and his biographical data on the back.

Selling a consumable product with baseball cards was not new; the American Tobacco Company and Goudy Chewing Gum had done it years before.

Berger took his baseball card idea to Topps. Because he wasn't confident the cards would sell beyond their first year, he recommended Topps issue them without a year designation. The first set was released at the start of the 1952 season. Berger's job was to go around the major leagues and secure contracts with players for permission to make their cards.

To Berger's surprise—and Topps'—the cards sold extremely well. As the 1952 season unfolded, kids everywhere were buying them. Recognizing they had a gold mine in the new market, Topps made a second series of cards with all new players and released it later in the year. Production was rushed to get the second series to retailers. But there were delays and by the time the cards were shipped out the baseball season was ending and kids' attention had shifted to football. As a result, the second series didn't sell and retailers sent boxes and boxes of unopened packs back to Topps for refunds.

Topps stockpiled the refunded cards in a New Jersey warehouse where they remained for several years. While they continued to release new cards every year, to get something—*anything*—for the 1952 cards, they tried selling the unopened packs at carnivals and fairs, but with little success. Boxes of cards—thousands of them—remained in storage collecting dust. Finally, in 1960, when Topps had to start paying for the storage, the company decided it was time to cut their losses and give up. The only value the cards had was a tax write-off as a business loss, so Berger was instructed to throw them all away. He rented a garbage scow and loaded it with cases of cards and pointed the pilot in the direction of the Atlantic Ocean. The scow steamed out to sea and from its deck Berger watched case after case get tossed overboard to their final resting place on the ocean floor.

But bubble gum trading cards had found a surprising market. They were a hit with Baby Boomer kids in the 1950's and '60's. They swapped player cards the same way major league teams traded players in those days, based on performance and not on their salaries or contract status. A star like Whitey Ford was worth a Hector Lopez *and* a Jackie Jensen. Duplicate cards of the same player—*doubles*—were unavoidable and many ended up clothes-pinned to the spokes of bicycles where they made an entertaining motorcycle sound. Games were invented, like flipping them on sidewalks and basement floors, and if your card landed face up and your friend's didn't, you claimed both cards. A card's condition meant something, but not as much as sentiment, as kids collected the cards of their favorite players and teams and bundled them together with rubber bands or stacked them in shoe boxes.

Cards and the sugary gum were sold in sealed packs for five cents. A kid would open a new pack by sliding his finger down the seal on the backside and letting the pack open like a clamshell. He was greeted by a brittle slab of gum on top of the first card. With the same joyful expectation of opening a Christmas present, he would thumb through the pack hoping to find his favorite player. All that joy for five cents.

Boomer kids had no idea that in the future some cards would be worth hundreds of times their original purchase price. Collecting cards was just a joy of kiddom. Then, inevitably they became teenagers and began to put away kid things like baseball cards and replace them with things that were more age-appropriate, like girls as my father had predicted. My story was a typical one. I stopped collecting cards in high school and after I went away to college my mother one day cleaned my bedroom closet of the childhood possessions I had outgrown, including a shoe box filled with my cards. Without consulting me, she tossed them out with the trash. It may not have been an ocean burial but was just as permanent.

After college I completely forgot about baseball cards. The business nosedived in the 1970's, but then came back slightly as the decade ended. In the 1980's everything changed. Interest in cards returned, this time taking off like a rocket. Card prices shot up. Boomers in their 30's had well-paying jobs with discretionary incomes for buying things they didn't need and nostalgia led them to the revived baseball card market.

The hobby of collecting cards was back in a big way, but now for a different reason: as investments. Cards became like stocks bought and sold for profit, and the prices of the oldest cards—the cards of Boomers' youth in the 1950's—were the greatest. A monthly magazine called Becket Price Guide was published to track their value for the new speculators. Collectors whose mothers had not trashed their shoe boxes of cards twenty years before discovered they were in possession of valuable gems from that age, like the cards of Willie Mays, Mickey Mantle, Hank Aaron, or Ted Williams. Some holding hundreds of valuable vintage cards opened shops in strip malls to sell them at or above Becket prices, and buyers were willing to bite. Of course, the highest card prices was reserved for those in mint condition, cards that had never come near a bicycle spoke. Dealers mounted them in rigid plastic cases and had them appraised under magnifying glasses like they were diamonds. They bought old cards, too, from Boomers who were dumping their collections, and then priced them to sell at even higher prices. But at *what* price? What was a 1958 Warren Spahn worth? Answer: whatever a buyer was willing to pay.

In this new market a player's highest priced card was his rookie card, his first card released at the start of his career. This made card buying truly like purchasing stocks, having to speculate which rookies were likely to become stars. What's more, new card manufacturers were getting into the market and speculators had to choose *whose* rookie card would be the best bet. Would Upper Deck's 1989 Ken Griffey rookie take off compared to his Topps rookie? (Answer: yes)

Upper Deck was a game changer, making cards of higher quality, printing them on heavy stock to assure crisp corners, with laser-sharp photos and a hologram on the back of each card to verify its authenticity and prove it wasn't counterfeit. Fake cards were out there in the new market, too.

Within a couple years all card manufacturers were making theirs from heavy, crisp-cornered stock instead of cheap cardboard. Card collecting was no longer a kid's pleasure. The cards were priced out of their allowance range. And the gum? The highly-sugared bubble gum could discolor and devalue any card it touched, so gum disappeared from the packs Topps was selling.

In the summer of 1991 I was curious enough about the new market to seek advice from a serious collector I knew. I asked him, *Whose card should I buy as a good investment?* Without hesitation, he replied a Topps 1982 Cal Ripken, his rookie card. Cal was in the middle of a Hall Of Fame career and having his best year yet, and getting close to breaking Lou Gehrig's record for consecutive games played. My collector friend said he had driven 300 miles (round trip) to Duluth that week to buy a dozen Ripken rookies for $10 apiece. *Buy now*, he advised me. I may have been curious, but I wasn't ambitious enough and passed on his advice. Two months later, as a birthday present, my wife bought me an '82 Ripken for $120.

This takes me back to the cards Topps dumped in the Atlantic Ocean.

Released as a second series in 1952, the cards that received the sea burial included lesser known players who had been bypassed in Topps' first series, players who were either rookies or early in their careers. Mickey Mantle was one of them. In 1960, the year the cases were dumped, Topps had no reason to expect that one day a '52 Mantle would become as valuable as priceless art. They may have known that the ocean treasure chest contained hundreds—or maybe thousands—of the first card of the player who had replaced Joe DiMaggio in centerfield at Yankee Stadium and was on his way to becoming a baseball idol, but they also knew it made no economic sense to bear the cost of storing all those worthless cards in a warehouse any longer. Of course, the fact that the value of a '52 Mantle card would skyrocket one day was due in part to Topp's decision to limit their supply to demanding investors by taking thousands out of circulation.

A 1952 Mickey Mantle—just *saying* a 1952 Mantle makes it sound like a vintage wine—became the highest priced baseball card in history. Supply and demand differences will do that. So does the legendary status Mantle had achieved and retained even after his death in 1995. But perhaps the biggest reason was the great number of obscenely rich collectors with thousands of dollars to burn and their view that rare baseball cards were legitimate assets to own and brag about.

Like with all cards, card quality affected the value of a '52 Mantle. In all the years a limited number of '52 Mantles had been in circulation, they received various standards of care. Some were babied behind glass, but many were stored in stacks held by rubber bands. Some may have been won or lost in card flips on basement floors. Regardless, anyone owning a '52 Mantle would one day rush to have theirs appraised, and even those who had been rough with theirs were ecstatic to get appraisals as high as $10,000.

Those that carried ratings of "Good to Near Mint" would sell as high as $250,000 at auctions.

A rating of "Near Mint to Mint-8"—and one day it was established that only 6 in the world had a rating that high—was worth as much as $1 million.

Unbelievable. But there's more.

Higher still was a "Mint 9" rating, of which there have been only three. They've sold as high as $7 million.

That's not the end.

One 1952 Mantle—and there has been *only* one—received a rating higher than Mint 9. It got a Mint 9.5. There has never been a 10. A Mint 9.5 has four perfectly sharp corners, not even a hint of a crease, good color, and an image that is centered perfectly on the card top-to-bottom and left-to-right. It is as close to perfection as a card can get, and it is something of a miracle that a card sold in 1952 could retain its pristine condition for 70 years. Only one has. And it sold for $12.6 million.

It's the Mona Lisa of baseball cards.

11

Only In Baseball

I f *Stranger Things* is your thing, here are two oddities that could only happen in baseball.

One, a player played for both teams in a Major League game, and *in the same inning*.

And two, a baserunner once stole first base.

On June 26, 2024, a game between the host Boston Red Sox and the visiting Toronto Blue Jays was postponed in the 2nd inning because of rain. Toronto catcher Danny Jansen was on-deck waiting to bat when the game was called. Later, it was announced that the game would continue as the first game of a double header to be played on August 26th, when Toronto would next visit Boston.

On July 27th Jansen was traded to Boston.

The game resumed where it had been halted, in the second inning with the same lineups for both teams. That meant Jansen, now sitting in the Red Sox dugout, was still in the Blue Jay lineup and due to bat right away. But before the first pitch it was announced that Jansen was being removed for a pinch hitter and that Boston's starting catcher was being replaced by Jansen. Both changes occurred in the second inning. In the same inning Jansen was removed from one lineup and placed in the other.

Toronto won the game 4-1. The box score for the game shows Jansen in the Blue Jay lineup with no official at-bats and in the Red Sox lineup going 1-for-4. It was a first in baseball history. The Hall of Fame in Cooperstown announced right away that Jansen and the game will be displayed in Cooperstown, along with a copy of the box score.

In a game played in 1908 the Cleveland Indians and Detroit Tigers were tied in the late innings, with the Tigers threatening to score, posting runners on first and third base. Future Hall-of-Famer Sam Crawford was at bat and the runner on first, a player named Germany Schaefer, a footnote in history compared to Crawford, flashed the signal to the runner on third, Davy Jones, for a double steal, a tactic often used in baseball in first-and-third situations to lure the catcher to throw to second so that the runner on third can score.

The Cleveland pitcher threw to the plate as Schaefer took off for second. But Cleveland's catcher didn't take the bait. Instead of trying to throw out Schaefer, he held onto the ball to leave Jones no choice but to stay on third base. Schaefer arrived safely at second.

Now Detroit had runners on second and third. Schaefer reportedly yelled to Jones, "Let's try it again," and on the next pitch raced *back to first* in an attempt to draw the catcher's throw, figuring if he didn't throw to second, maybe he would throw to first.

But nothing happened. The catcher still held the ball. Schaefer had—what? Stolen first base? All the players on the field, including Jones were stunned. Nobody moved, including Cleveland's first baseman. He hadn't bothered to rush forward and cover the bag. Umpires convened and talked amongst themselves and decided it was legal.

Now, Detroit had runners on first and third again by virtue of Schaefer successfully stealing second *and* first base, in that order, completely within the rules of the game. There has never been a play like this in professional football or basketball, in which a player has reversed himself intentionally, running or dribbling backwards, or shooting at his own basket, as a tactic to win a game. Only in baseball could a backwards play like this make sense.

On the next pitch, Schaefer stole second again, this time drawing a throw from the beleaguered Cleveland catcher, and Jones scampered home with the go-ahead run.

Schaefer had a reputation for being a trickster and reportedly attempted similar steals of first base in other games, too. But baseball got in the last word. After his death in 1920, a rule was added to the game, Rule 5.09(b)(10), that states a base runner is out if, after having acquired legal possession of a base, he runs the bases in reverse order for the purpose of confusing the defense or *making a travesty of the game.*

It's the Schaefer rule. It's too bad. The game is more fun if it contains antics like Schaefer's.

TORONTO 4, BOSTON 1 (G1)

TORONTO	AB	R	H	BI	BB	SO	Avg.
Bichette ss	1	0	0	0	0	1	.222
Serven c	3	1	1	0	0	0	.159
Horwitz 2b-1b	4	0	0	0	0	2	.255
Clement pr-3b	0	1	0	0	0	0	.265
Guerrero 1b-3b	3	1	1	2	1	1	.320
Turner dh	1	0	0	0	0	0	.256
Barger ph-dh	3	0	1	1	0	2	.197
Springer rf	4	1	1	1	0	1	.220
Schneider lf	3	0	1	0	1	2	.199
Loperfido lf	0	0	0	0	0	0	.239
D.Jansen c	0	0	0	0	0	0	.233
Varsho ph-cf	4	0	1	0	0	1	.218
Kiner-Falefa 3b	0	0	0	0	0	0	.292
Wagner ph-2b	4	0	0	0	0	2	.282
Kiermaier cf	0	0	0	0	0	0	.195
Jimenez ss	4	0	0	0	0	1	.222
TOTALS	**34**	**4**	**6**	**4**	**2**	**13**	
BOSTON	**AB**	**R**	**H**	**BI**	**BB**	**SO**	**Avg.**
Duran cf	4	1	1	1	0	1	.289
Hamilton ss-2b	2	0	0	0	0	1	.251
Gonzalez ph-2b	2	0	1	0	0	0	.278
Abreu rf	1	0	0	0	1	0	.268
O'Neill ph-rf	1	0	0	0	1	0	.261
Devers 3b	4	0	0	0	0	1	.290
Refsnyder lf	4	0	0	0	0	2	.286
Yoshida dh	4	0	1	0	0	1	.292
Valdez 2b	0	0	0	0	0	0	.224
D.Jansen c	4	0	1	0	0	1	.233
Smith 1b	0	0	0	0	0	0	.237
Casas 1b	2	0	0	0	1	2	.270
McGuire c	0	0	0	0	0	0	.209
Rafaela ss	3	0	0	0	0	2	.259
TOTALS	**31**	**1**	**4**	**1**	**3**	**11**	

Toronto	000 000 130 —	4	6	0
Boston	000 000 010 —	1	4	2

12

Danger On The Basepaths

"There are no dragons in baseball, only shortstops."
— A. Bartlett Giamatti, former MLB
Commissioner

I learned how to keep score at a baseball game from instructions I read in a Washington Senators gameday program in 1959. In the years since I've revised the method the program taught me. My revisions have had a goal: to record enough detail so that someday I can recreate the entire game and every play that happened, not just how many runs a team scored and *who* scored them, but *how* they were scored.

Here's my method.

A scorecard has a nine-by-nine grid of squares for each team. To the left of the grid is a column of players, the team's batting order, with each player's on-field position coded as a number. The pitcher and catcher are numbers 1 and 2, respectively. Who's On First—the first baseman—is #3. What's On Second is #4. I Don't Know, the third baseman, is #5. And so on.

The nine columns in the grid represent the game's nine innings. Hence, what the leadoff batter does in the first inning is recorded in the square on the top line under the first column. If the clean-up hitter leads off the second inning, what he does is recorded in Row 4—his line—under the second column.

When a batter makes an out, how he went out gets a unique designation. Strikeouts are marked as K's. Upside down K's are for *called* strikeouts.

If a batter flies out, the coded position of the player who caught the fly is noted in the square. From left to right, outfielders are 7, 8, and 9. Shortstops are 6. When a batter grounds out, the position numbers of the players who handled the ball go in the square. A groundout to short is denoted as 6-3. If the pitcher covers first on a groundout hit to the first baseman, it's 3-1.

Still with me?

What I've described so far is more or less universal. But here's where my method veers off into statistical geekdom.

I treat each square in the grid like it's an infield. First base is in the lower right hand corner. Second base is upper right. Third is upper left and home is lower left. Going around the square counter-clockwise is like circling the bases.

With my method I wish to record how a runner advances from base to base, and for that I use the corners of the square.

Example.

Let's say a batter—we'll call him Rod Carew—draws a walk. A "W" is placed in the lower righthand corner of Carew's square, denoting he got to first base on a walk. The next batter—say it's leftfielder Larry Hisle—singles and Carew advances to 3rd. In Carew's upper left corner—i.e., 3rd base—Larry's position number—a "7"—is entered to indicate Larry was the batter who got Carew there. In fact, a '7' goes there regardless of *how* Larry got Carew to third. It could have been a groundball or a flyout, or an error. But in this case Larry singled. So a (/)—the symbol for a single—is placed in Larry's lower right corner.

At this point my scorecard shows Carew on 3rd and Hisle on 1st and how they got there.

The next batter is catcher Butch Wynegar. As the catcher, he is identified as position #2. Butch doubles, indicated by a > extending to the top right corner of Butch's square.

Carew scores. I place a "2" in the lower left hand corner of his square, which is home plate, but I *circle* it, meaning he scored a run. Hisle advances to 3rd. A "2"—again, representing Wynegar—goes in the 3rd base spot in Hisle's square.

What if a runner advances on a wild pitch? Answer: WP.

Batter reaches base on an error by the shortstop? E-6. It goes in the lower right corner if he stopped at first base.

Home run? An enclosed diamond.

A triple? A diamond with only three sides showing.

And what about a rare play? What if a runner on 3rd is thrown out at home trying to score on a sacrifice fly? And, say the flyball was hit to the left fielder. Then, in the runner's lower left corner—home plate—I enter the numbers 7-2. Out at home. Thrown out by #7.

Those are the basics.

Now, here is a scorecard example for a real game I attended.

It was the second game in the 2023 American League Wild Card Series in which the Minnesota Twins beat the Toronto Blue Jays, 2-0. It was an important game, and by winning the Twins advanced to meet the Houston Astros in the divisional series.

The game was scoreless for the first three innings. Starting pitchers Sonny Gray for the Twins and Jose Berrios for the Blue Jay were sharp and efficient at getting batters out. My scorecard says that Berrios threw only 39 pitches in three innings. Yes, I record pitch counts, too.

In the bottom of the 4th Berrios walked the Twins leadoff hitter Royce Lewis on 8 pitches. I placed a "W" in the lower right corner of Royce's 4th-inning square.

I don't record the number of pitches thrown to a particular hitter, just total pitches in an inning, but in this case I had sketched a dashed line beneath Lewis's square to mean that Berrios was removed from the game and wouldn't pitch to the next batter, and as he left the mound I checked the stadium scoreboard to note that his pitch count was 47. Berrios had thrown a total of 47 pitches, meaning he had thrown 8 to Lewis.

They're taking Berrios out after only 47 pitches! Holy s—!

Like others seated around me in Section T, I was stunned. Not only had Berrios thrown only 47 pitches, he had fanned five Twins. He was giving the Twins fits. *We can't hit him today,* I thought. And he's still fresh. What a break for us! Even from my distant view in Section T, I could see Berrios was furious leaving the mound for the dugout. I placed a question mark next to the dashed line under Lewis's walk. It was my way of recording disbelief at what the Toronto manager had done.

With reliever Yusei Kikuchi in Berrios' place, the Twins scored twice. The Twins had taken a 2-0 lead, thanks, in my opinion, to the Toronto manager for yanking Berrios so soon.

In the top of the 5th Toronto threatened to score. They had runners on 2nd and 3rd—first baseman Vladimir Guerrero and outfielder George Springer—with two outs. My scorecard says how they got there.

With one out, Springer singled. I put a (/) in his lower right corner.

The next batter was Brandon Belt. Sonny Gray struck him out. I wrote a K in his square. Two outs.

Guerrero walked. I placed a "W" in his lower right corner. In Springer's upper right, I wrote "3", meaning he reached 2nd base as a result of what Guerrero (#3) did with his at bat.

Next, Twins catcher Ryan Jeffers let a passed ball get by him and both runners advanced one base. I wrote "PB" in two places: Springer's upper left corner and Guerrero's upper right.

With runners on 2nd and 3rd, Toronto's clean-up hitter Bo Bichette came to bat. Bichette was already two-for-two in the game, having singled twice. The situation looked dire for Sonny Gray and the Twins.

But my scorecard doesn't show that Bichette batted in the 5th inning. Instead, he led off the 6th and struck out. What my scorecard *does* show in the 5th inning are a pair of numbers inside Guerrero's square, the numbers 1-6, meaning Guerrero was picked off by the pitcher throwing to the shortstop for the third out of the inning, Sonny Gray to Carlos Correa.

It was a beautiful play that was magnificently timed, and a game saver. Since that day, whenever I glance at the scorecard and note the pair of numbers 1-6, the pickoff play comes back to me in a wonderful memory.

The memory is strengthened by what I read in the sports section the next day, that the pickoff was Correa's idea. Earlier in the game, the article said, he had told Gray the crowd noise was so loud Blue Jay baserunners couldn't hear the warnings of their base coaches. He said a pickoff play might work. Correa, Gray, and catcher Jeffers had a series of signals for a pickoff, starting with Correa flashing a sign to Jeffers that the play was on, a play they called "timing pick" because it involved precise timing between the pitcher and shortstop to work. When Correa saw the large lead Guerrero was taking from 2nd base, he gave the signal to Jeffers and Jeffers relayed the signal to Gray. Correa snuck in behind Guerrero, who, just as Correa had predicted, didn't hear the warning of the third base coach and thus didn't move until he saw Gray spin around when it was too late. Gray threw and Correa tagged Guerrero as he slid into the base. The crowd roared. It was beautiful.

In the 9th inning I got up from my seat to stand and watch the end of the game from behind Section T. When the Blue Jay's Matt Chapman struck out for the second out in the inning, I marked a "K" on my scorecard. One out to go.

Then, I heard someone standing next to me ask, "What does your scorecard say about the game?"

I looked over to see a man wearing a Blue Jays jersey.

"What?" I asked.

He pointed to the third base line on the field.

"The play that won the game for the Twins," he said bitterly. He was referring to a line drive Chapman had hit in the 6th inning with the bases loaded. It landed foul by a foot. Had it been fair, two runs—and maybe three—would have scored and the game would have turned out differently.

"I don't score foul balls," I said with a smile.

I pointed to what my scorecard said. Chapman's at-bat in the 6th was marked with a 6-4-3 notation, meaning he had hit into a double play started by shortstop Correa. The play had ended the inning and left the Blue Jays scoreless.

"My scorecard says something different," I said.

"Yeah, lucky for the Twins," he said.

"That's baseball."

"Lucky."

"Game of inches."

I flipped to the Twin's side of my scorecard. "But here's something important," I said, pointing to the question mark I had placed next to the walk Jose Berrios issued to Lewis to start the 4th inning, only to be taken out before facing another batter. "Your guy was killing us," I said. "Why in the world did your manager pull him? We couldn't hit Berrios. That move was a critical mistake. Don't you think?"

The Blue Jay fan nodded with a disdainful smirk.

I turned to the Blue Jay scorecard again and pointed to the 5th inning. 1-6. Gray to Correa. The pickoff of Guerrero. "But this…" I said. "This was *huge*. *This* decided the game for the Twins." And he had to agree with me again. "It was beautiful baseball," I finished.

Baserunning—good and bad—makes baseball fun to watch. It's part of the game's explosive action that often decides the outcome of a game. It can be scary for runners. It's dangerous out there on the basepaths and runners find comfort standing safely at a base, even if just for a moment. They lead off warily and take enormous risks trying to advance. But advance they must. It's a long way to circle the bases and arrive home safely starting from first base.

In his philosophical musing *Take Time For Paradise*, former Major League commissioner A. Bartlett Giamatti writes about what circling the bases means to the game. He asks why home plate isn't called fourth base and answers the question himself. Home is a concept, he writes, a state of mind in which one learns to be separate but remains also as the place where a reunion will occur. In baseball, a batter starts at home but hopes to return there.

Giamatti likens a baserunner to the legendary Odysseus in the *Odyssey*, on a homeward journey full of turnings, wanderings, and danger. "To attempt to go home," Giamatti writes, "is to go the long way around, to stray and separate in the hope of finding completeness in reunion." When a baserunner doesn't make it around to score, he is said to have *died* on base. "There are no dragons in baseball," Giamatti goes on, "only shortstops, but they can emerge from nowhere to cut one down."

13

The Sandlot

"Third base was Eddie's old shirt,
Second was Schmidt's Chevrolet.
I had a sure double
And was just rounding first
When Schmidt's Mom drove second away."
—John McCutcheon, *Baseball On The Block*

Baseball is a kid's game and kids play it everywhere, not just on groomed ballfields. They'll find an empty space and use stones and pieces of cardboard and their jackets for bases to make an infield. They might play with three bases, or five, or six. Or *none*. A version played on narrow New York streets called stickball has *no bases* at all. It's called stickball because the kids use sawed-off broomsticks or mop handles as bats. So as to not break the windows of houses lining both sides of the street a tennis ball or rubber ball replaces a real baseball.

There is a famous photograph of Willie Mays in a white shirt and dark trousers playing stickball on a city street. A broom handle is cocked behind his head and a big smile fills his familiar face. He was a New York Giant at the time and perhaps the Polo Grounds was only a few blocks away. The picture says something to me, that baseball is a kid's game and there's still a kid living in a major league star.

The Sandlot is a kid movie, and a great baseball movie, too. It's a story about how kids turn an empty lot into a makeshift ballfield where they play every day in the summer. The movie doesn't deal with winning and losing and doesn't have to. It's about something bigger, which is kids playing baseball just for the fun of it, not in an organized league with umpires, or coaches arguing with umpires, or parents arguing with coaches. It's a coming-of-age story about how they use the sandlot as a proving ground for themselves in the absence of adults. In that way, *The Sandlot* is a lot like a Peanuts comic strip, with no grown-ups in the story to mess things up.

The movie is about boys' dreams. For Benny The Jet Rodriguez, it's playing in the major leagues for the Los Angeles Dodgers. For Michael Squints Palledorous it's planting a sloppy kiss on the lips of Wendy Peffercorn, the public swimming pool lifeguard with whom he is infatuated, in one of the movie's side stories about what else boys experience growing up. The story includes a mystery about a beast living beyond the sandlot's outfield fence where the boys' homerun balls land. When they finally solve the mystery, they not only get their baseballs back, but discover a friendship on the other side of the fence that the audience knows will contribute to their growing up.

But mostly it's about the sandlot and what it means to them. At the sandlot they don't practice or play by rigid schedules wearing uniforms. They just show up and play. They are the commissioners, managers and umpires of their games and get to make the rules. They pool their loose change to buy a new ball when they lose their old one. They don't pick sides or keep score either, but play a game that goes on and on, inning after inning. In that way, they have eliminated all time constraints on their game.

Baseball is depicted in *The Sandlot* as possessing magic. Scotty, the brainy newcomer who joins the game with no baseball skills, is assigned on his first day to play "left-center" without knowing where it is or how to catch a flyball. He asks Benny to teach him and Benny, after struggling with a question he's never been asked before, points to left-center and tells Scotty to stand there and when he sees the ball coming at him simply hold his glove up in the air and he'll be fine. Then, to test his advice, Benny hits him a fly and Scotty does as he is told, standing motionless and holding his pancake mitt high over his head with his eyes shut as he mutters a prayerful wish. We watch the ball descend in slow motion from the top of its arc to land securely in the pocket of

Scotty's mitt. It's magic, and enough of a lesson for Scotty to become a pretty good ballplayer after that.

In another scene the boys play a 4th of July night game under the lights of exploding fireworks. "Baseball is life," Benny reminds the others. While the other boys stare wide-eyed at the pyrotechnics in the sky, we see Benny silhouetted in the fireworks glow circling the bases, head down, in a home-run trot he learned from watching the Dodgers play.

One day Scotty hits a home run over the fence into the domain of the beast. He tearfully confesses that he took the ball from his stepfather's trophy shelf and pleads with the other boys' to help him get it back. They just laugh. *Forget it,* they say. The beast has it now. Then, Scotty tells them the ball had an autograph from somebody, somebody named…Baby…no Babe…Babe Ruth. The others boys scream at him. *Babe Ruth!* That changes everything and they proceed to make a series of desperate attempts to retrieve the ball. The beast foils them every time. They lose hope. Then, one night in his bedroom, Benny gets a visit from Babe Ruth's ghostly visage who tells him, "Remember, kid. There's heroes and there's legends. Heroes get remembered but legends never die." After the ghost fades away, Benny knows he has to be the one to confront the beast.

The sandlot is not permanent in the boys' lives. Baseball has brought them together but one day they will grow up and baseball on the sandlot will become just a wonderful memory of a special time for them. I love the movie's ending in which we see them tossing a ball to each other and disappearing one-by-one while the story's narrator—Scotty as an adult—tells us what happened to them in their grown-up lives after they moved away. Some had successful careers. Squints and Wendy got married and raised nine kids. And Benny, the legend who taught Scotty the game and got his Babe Ruth ball back, went on to play for the Dodgers.

Kids don't have sandlots anymore. Vacant lots don't exist in city neighborhoods. They're too valuable for their absentee owners to leave empty. They aren't interested in allowing their property to become a public place enjoyed by others.

In the neighborhood where I grew up there was a sandlot where me and my friends laid out a baseball diamond. We used flat pieces of wood for bases. There was no mound or backstop or foul lines. The infield was scattered patches of grass and weeds, and in left field there was a shallow ditch too far to be reached with a homerun but a ball rolling into it was declared a ground-rule *triple*. Rightfield had an eight-foot wooden fence that extended from the foul line to straightaway center—we called it the *Brown Monster*—and could be cleared by a well-tagged fly ball, particularly one hit close to the foul line. On rare occasions a homerun flew over it to land in a backyard on the other side.

The year before I went away to college the sandlot was taken from us. A billboard was erected with the name of a new neighborhood and a map of numbered lots. One day a bulldozer showed up to move dirt around and stakes with ribbons were pounded in the ground. A paved street was rolled out and *For Sale* signs went up. Then houses were built. The sandlot—our ballfield—had been turned into a cul-de-sac for a dozen homes and, just as the kids in the movie experienced, became a memory for me and my friends.

But in truth there was another reason we lost it. But more about that later.

I lived a block from the sandlot—the cul-de-sac—starting when I was eight until I went away to college. I came home for holidays and summer vacations. In those days my family observed a Christmas tradition every year that on the Friday night before Christmas we would go house-to-house caroling through the neighborhood. My mother and father were the organizers. There was one year in particular I remember caroling. Not to spoil the story, but it was the year my sandlot story got some closure.

I was in my second year of college and I came home for the holidays on the day we would carol. When I walked in the front door I found my parents sitting at the kitchen table arranging copies of the hymns we would sing, setting aside some for the neighbors who would be joining us.

"Who'd you get a ride with?" my father asked me.

"Tommy," I answered, opening the refrigerator door. "I asked him if he wanted to join us and he said no. He missed his girlfriend."

"And you didn't?" my mother asked.

"Of course, I did." I reached down and gave her a hug. "But now I'm home."

"Smooth," my father said.

After dinner the carolers assembled in front of our house. We stood on the sidewalk and greeted each other wearing winter coats and scarves and stocking caps and admired the galaxy of Christmas lights on both sides of Sycamore Street. My father delivered his customary pre-carol pep talk. "Remember what we're doing tonight," he said. "We're taking a solemn oath to bring the good news. Tonight, we are the Lord's angels announcing Christ's birth."

My mother humored him. "Okay," she said to the group, "everyone follow Gabriel."

We would sing to every house on the block. Down one side and then the other. Fourteen hymns for fourteen houses, two hours at the most, including time to accept invitations from some neighbors to come inside for refreshments and a chance to warm up, which for the adults meant their insides, too. At most houses, porch lights would come on and neighbors would step outside for a few chilly minutes to enjoy their personal carol and then thank us with shouts of Merry Christmas when we were done.

We sang "O Come All Ye Faithful" to the Spencers and "Hark the Herald Angels Sing" to the Schmidts, who invited us inside for hot chocolate and cookies before sending us on our way again. We crossed the street and sang to the Taylors, "On Jordan's Bank the Baptist's Cry", a favorite of my mother's.

Not all our neighbors were welcoming. Frank Brophy, the eighth neighbor on the route, was a prime example. Every year he stayed inside while we sang in front of his house. He was always home, a light always shone in his living room, but he wouldn't come to the door. He never had. And presumably never would.

For many years Frank Brophy had been at odds with the neighbors. He was friendly enough standing in his driveway and waving to passers-by, but he refused invitations to his neighbors' parties and other gatherings, usually without an RSVP. *Keeps to himself* was an apt description of him. Nobody knew much about him, other than he was a widower living alone. There were rumors he was a drinker.

What was certain was that he complained about everything, about parked cars in front of his house, loose dogs, creeping crabgrass, and noises after dark. Things were worse for the kids in the neighborhood. Frank Brophy had no tolerance for kids riding their bikes in his driveway or running across his lawn or playing ball in the street. Over the years, by my count, Frank Brophy had seized a half-dozen footballs that bounced errantly into his front yard, a kite that crashed-landed on his roof, and Tommy Harrell's remote-controlled race car that veered off course to make an unplanned pit stop in Brophy's open garage. The boys on Sycamore Street retaliated with acts of vandalism, using weapons like soap, toilet paper, and raw eggs. We scribbled threatening messages on his sidewalk and discovered that while chalk disappears in the rain, spray paint does not. That happened the year we were particularly nasty. My father made us scrub the concrete clean again with wire brushes.

The carolers moved to the front of Brophy's darkened porch and sang "Silent Night". When we were done my father complained it was a waste of Christmas's best hymn and then stomped off to the next house. After a pause to see if Brophy would make a surprise appearance on his porch, the caroling crew followed. I held back for another moment, my thoughts awash with the memories of long-ago battles with Frank Brophy.

And a secret I had been keeping from my parents about my last crime against Brophy.

It happened four years before and involved the sandlot.

Behind Brophy's house was the new cul-de-sac where the sandlot used to be. The rightfield fence—the *Brown Monster*—was directly behind his backyard. In its day, a lot of doubles and triples had caromed off the fence, and only a few homeruns had cleared it to land in Brophy's yard. I hit one once. Once. Mine was the last hit in the last game we played on the sandlot before we switched to a field at the high school almost a mile away.

I tagged one of Charlie Spencer's hanging curves and hit a deep fly ball down the foul line. All eyes were on the ball's arcing flight as right fielder Tommy Harrell raced back until he ran out of room and stopped to watch the ball sail twenty feet over his head and the fence.

Touch them all, my teammates hollered.

I waved my arms and was about to start my home run trot when we all heard it: a loud crash and the unmistakable sound of broken glass sprinkling on wood, presumably Brophy's backyard deck.

I didn't touch them all. I didn't touch any base. As soon as we realized what had happened, we all reached for our bats and gloves and scattered like mice. We raced across the street and kept going, leaving the lot empty without a clue of the game left behind. It was the last baseball game ever played on the sandlot. We never told our parents why we stopped and vowed to never utter a word about what had happened to anyone. If it was discussed at all among us, usually in a whisper, the incident was referred to as the *unsolved crime*.

I ran to catch up with the other carolers.

Next, we sang "We Three Kings Of Orient Are" to the Fitzpatricks and then went inside for hot cider and Tom and Jerrys. There were four houses left on the block when I suddenly realized I had dropped a glove somewhere and told the others not to wait for me as I retreated to find it. With a flashlight my father gave me I retraced my steps on the sidewalk. In front of Brophy's house, with my flashlight beam and eyes directed downward, I heard a voice.

"Was it the left hand?"

Startled, I looked up to see a shadowed figure on Brophy's front porch.

"What?"

"I asked if it was a left hand. The glove you're looking for."

It was Frank Brophy.

"Yeah. I dropped it here somewhere."

Brophy raised his arm. "I got it right here."

I froze, uncertain what to do next. In my mind I saw my entire childhood as a series of misdirected flights of footballs, baseballs, and kites, the only things that up until that moment had connected my life with Frank Brophy's. Now a glove. The boys of Sycamore Street used to speculate what Brophy did with all the stuff he took from us. Did he throw it out with the trash? Did he build a shrine in a spare bedroom to showcase the spoils of his wars with us?

Cautiously, I approached the house. I was about to say thanks when Frank Brophy asked, "So, how do you like college?"

Stunned by the question, I hesitated before answering, "Fine. It's good."

"Glad to hear it. You're in your second year, right?"

"Yeah....second year."

"Say, I've got something for you. Why don't you come inside for a minute?"

I stopped breathing. I had never set foot inside the House of Brophy. In our youth, besides the talk of a shrine of stolen kid stuff, my friends and I imagined rooms inside decorated like scenes from an Edgar Allan Poe tale, tributes to horror, a pit and a pendulum in the basement or a raven in a cage. Kids believed in those things.

But I accepted Brophy's invitation and followed him inside.

The house was warm and the living room was small, crowded by a card table around which three middle-aged men sat. On the table were knives and pieces of plastic, brushes, and tubes of paint and glue.

The men looked up, and one of them asked, "Who's your friend, Frank?"

"This is Ted. He lives across the street. He's one of the carolers."

"Well, then," a second man said," I have to ask you, Frank. What kind of a friend doesn't get up to go outside and listen to him sing?"

"I could hear them okay," Brophy replied. "Silent Night. Maybe next Christmas we'll *all* go outside and listen."

"Frank, Frank, Frank.." the man continued, "every year it's the same excuse. What do we have to do? *Push* you out the door?"

"Anyway," Brophy said, "I invited Ted to come in because I have a gift for him."

"Ted, take off your coat and stay awhile," the third man said. "There's egg nog in the kitchen and we could use a hand."

"What are you guys doing?" I asked, looking at the table.

"Making Christmas ornaments. We give them to the homeless shelter and orphanage."

"Ted has lived across the street his whole life," Brophy said. "Now he's in college. Studying to be an engineer."

"Is that so? Well, Ted, how about doing some engineering for us? We're pretty good with our hands but terrible at design. We're making too many stars and angels. Got any ideas?"

"I don't know," I answered, shrugging. "Maybe people in a homeless shelter would like an ornament that's a house, like the one they hope to have someday. Can you make little houses, maybe houses decorated for Christmas?"

"We can make *anything*," was the reply. "Ralph, why don't you turn your inn into a rambler? Put a wreath on it. Nobody's going to guess it's supposed to be an inn."

"Why don't you stay and help us?" Brophy asked, handing me a paper bag.

"Thanks, but I should get back and join the others. And thanks for finding my glove." I held up the bag. "And the gift."

"Well, you're welcome to come back after the caroling is done," Brophy said. "We've got a long night ahead of us."

We exchanged goodbyes and I went outside. I ran to catch up with the carolers in front of the last house, the Hartman's, next door to ours. We sang, "Joy to the World" and called it a night.

Back home, I sat at the kitchen table and opened the bag and peered inside.

"What is it, Ted?" my mother asked. "What did Frank give you?"

I reached in and pulled out an odd-looking piece of plastic, a cylinder with glass on the sides, and....*what was it?*

It was a Christmas ornament. Handmade. It was a glass cylinder with tiny garlands and ribbons glued all around the outside. And mounted inside....a baseball. But it wasn't a new one. It was bruised and some of its stitches were frayed and loose.

I held it up and turned it. I stared at the baseball inside the glass. And something else.

I remembered. The sandlot. The last homerun. The last game.

"Frank Brophy made that?" my mother asked. "Well, isn't that something. Where do you suppose he got the idea? Here, let me see it." In slow motion, I handed it to her.

"My, that's wonderful," my mother said, spinning the ornament. My father looked over her shoulder.

"Well, look at that," he said. "The glass is cracked. That's too bad. You didn't drop it, did you, Ted?"

I didn't hear my father. I wasn't listening. I was still lost in a sandlot memory. I stared at the ornament with glazed eyes.

"Ted?" my father repeated. "What's the matter?"

A smile crept across my face, small at first, but growing until it hung ear to ear. I thought about calling Tommy Harrell. He wouldn't believe this. "Nothing," I said. "It's okay."

"What a nice gift," said my mother. She went to the living room and found a place to hang the ornament on the tree. My father put his arm on her shoulder and said, "I guess Frank knew how much Ted likes baseball." Together, they admired the gift. "Ted," he asked, "are you sure you didn't drop it?"

I went to the front door and as I closed it behind me heard my father ask, "Ted? Where are you going?"

I didn't answer him. I stood on the front step and looked across the street. On Frank Brophy's front porch, the light had been turned on.

14

Baseball And Math

Wins Above Replacement =WAR = (Batting Runs + Base Running Runs + Fielding Runs + Positional Adjustment + League Adjustment +Replacement Runs) / (Runs Per Win)

Baseball and Math are great partners. They are inseparable. Think of all the stats! Think of all the numbers!

I learned how to calculate an earned run average at a young age. One day I figured out slugging percentages, and next came OPS (on base percentage *plus* slugging). WAR? Wins Above Replacement? The theory behind WAR makes sense but its equation is too complex to know if it's accurate. Babe Ruth had a career WAR of 183. A good player today has a single-season WAR of 8 or 9.

wRC+? Runs created, weighted for ballpark and era? Wow. The concept is good, that games are won by scoring runs and not by hitters getting on base. But in baseball's attempt to find the best method for measuring a player's worth, don't we have too many measures today? Is wRC+ one too many?

It's best just to leave player comparisons to raw data, knowing that a .400 batting average is twice as many hits as a .200 average.

But the probability of hitting .400. What is that?

Here's the math behind it.

The chances of something happening in baseball is all about probability, from P=0 (it never happens) to P=1 (it happens every time). If the probability of something happening is P, then the probability of it *not* happening is 1-P. If P = 0.400, then 1-P = 0.600.

But how do probabilities combine?

Take, for example, the probability (P) that Joe DiMaggio would hit safely in 56 consecutive games, which he did in 1941. It is considered to be such a monumental feat it may never be matched. What is the probability of it being matched? What was the probability of Joe doing it?

The calculation involves the probabilities of two independent events. The first is whether or not Joe would get a hit in any single game and the second is the probability of him stringing together enough games with hits until he got to 56.

During his streak Joe hit for an average of .408. That means for every at bat during his streak his probability of getting a hit was .408. His probability of making an out was 1.000 minus 0.408, or 0.592.

$$\mathbf{x} = 1.000. -0.408 = 0.592$$

"$\mathbf{x}$" is the probability Joe would make an out with each at bat.

The probability of him making two outs in a row is calculated by the square of $\mathbf{x}$, $\mathbf{x}^2$, or 0.592 x 0.592. It's like the probability of flipping a coin twice and having it come up heads both times. The probability of heads on one flip is 50/50, or ½, one out of two. The probability of it happening again is ½ x ½, or ¼, meaning one out of four, .25. Three heads in a row? ½ x ½ x ½, or 1/8.

Similarly, the probability of Joe making an out three times in a row is calculated by the cube of $\mathbf{x}$, $\mathbf{x}^3$, or 0.592 x 0.592 x 0.592. = 0.2075

During the streak Joe had an average of 3.98 at bats per game. In other words, the odds he would have no safe hits in a game were:

$$\mathbf{y} = (0.592)^{3.98} = 0.1241$$

and the probability he would get one or more safe hits in a game, $\mathbf{z}$, was equal to 1.000 − $\mathbf{y}$, or :

$$\mathbf{z} = 1.000 − 0.1241 = 0.8759$$

Which is pretty good, except that's for just one game.

Remember, the probability of Joe hitting safely in 56 games involves the probability of two independent events, **z** being one of the them. That's for one game. The other is the probability of **z** occurring in 56 straight games. The odds of Joe hitting safely in two consecutive games are calculated by the square of **z**, z^2, or 0.8759 x 0.8759, like the odds of two consecutive heads when flipping a coin. Call this P_2

$P_2 = (0.8759)^2 = .7672$ (the probability of Joe hitting safely in two consecutive games)

The odds of getting a hit in three consecutive games is the cube of **z**, z^3, or 0.8759 x 0.8759 x 0.8759. Call this P_3. And so on.

The probability of Joe hitting safely in 56 consecutive games—call it P_{56}—is calculated as

$P_{56} = (0.8759)^{56} = .0006$

And there's the answer, the odds Joe overcame when he set the record of hitting in 56 straight games . This is comparable to the odds of flipping a coin and having it come up heads eleven times in a row, ½ x ½ x ½, x ½, etc..

When Joe hit safely in 56 consecutive games, he was overcoming a probability of .0006, or, in other words, the odds *against* him were 1,667 to 1.

What if Joe had added one more game to his streak? What is P_{57}? It's $(0.8759)^{57} = .0005$. 2,000 to 1.

Does this mean the odds of a player breaking DiMaggio's streak are .0005? They are if he can hit .408 for 57 games. The problem for modern hitters to match DiMaggio are many, one being specialized relief pitching. Hitters don't face starting pitchers that last 7 to 8 innings like they did in 1941 and seldom do pitchers go through an opposing team's batting order more than twice. Even when hitters start seeing the opposing team's bullpen as early as the 4th or 5th inning they don't face any reliever more than once.

Add the greater variety of pitches today, having to play more night games, and opposing teams keeping data about a hitter's patterns and weaknesses, and it's highly unlikely that a player today can carry a batting average of .408 during a hitting streak that lasts two months. But if he hits well enough during a streak to keep up an average of, say, .350, which is fifty points lower than Joe during his streak, and if he came up to bat 3.92 times in a game, his P_{57} would be calculated as follows:

$$\mathbf{x} = 1.000 - 0.350 = 0.650$$
$$\mathbf{y} = (0.650)^{3.92} = 0.180$$
$$\mathbf{z} = 1.000 - 0.180 = 0.820$$
$$P_{57} = (.820)^{57} = .000012$$

Hitting in 57 straight games is to overcome odds of 83,000 to 1.

The odds that someone will break DiMaggio's record are 40 times harder today than in 1941.

That's enough math. Class dismissed.

15

Poets And Other Scriveners

"Say it ain't true, Roy."
—Bernard Malamud, from *The Natural*

Why is baseball the most literary of sports? Why does the game attract the attention of so many good writers? And not just sportswriters, but renowned authors and poets from outside the brotherhood of scribes. It's not by chance or circumstance, but I think it's because writers see baseball as something unique, a distinctly American game with opportunities for allegories about the American Dream and what it encompasses: ambition, success, greed, suffering, and failure. Loyalty and love. And broken hearts. Baseball is too central to our culture to *not* write about it. Baseball has given our lexicon more terms, phrases and idioms than any other sport. We give each other *rain checks*. We *play ball* when we cooperate. We *touch base* with each other and get ideas that come *out of left field*.

For some, baseball was all they ever wrote about, and to resounding acclaim. Roger Kahn's *Boys Of Summer* and the essays of Roger Angel are among the best writing you'll find about any sport. Columnist Thomas Boswell devoted his career with the *Washington Post* to baseball and once wrote a piece titled *99 Reasons Why Baseball Is Better Than Football*. The fiction of W.P. Kinsella, author of *Shoeless Joe*, the novel on which the movie *Field Of Dreams* was based, treats baseball with magical realism. And for many writing about baseball was a detour in their distinguished careers as authors of great fiction in general, Bernard Malamud and Philip Roth and John Updike. I could go on and on.

Poets, too.

In *Fathers Playing Catch With Sons,* his book of essays on sports, Donald Hall shared something he discovered in an autobiography of a poet named Alfred Kreymborg, who had written about another poet, Marianne Moore, one of great acclaim herself. The two poets were living in New York at the time, around 1913.

Kreymborg was well acquainted with Moore's reputation as someone who knew more about any subject in the world than anyone. To introduce her to baseball, a subject he was certain Moore knew nothing about, Kreymborg invited her to see a game with him at the Polo Grounds. The New York Giants were playing the Chicago Cubs and the great Christy Mathewson was pitching for the Giants.

When Mathewson threw a strike on his first pitch, Moore exclaimed, "Excellent." Kreymborg turned to her to ask if she knew who the pitcher was.

"I've never seen him before," she answered, "but I take it must be Mr. Mathewson."

At that moment Kreymborg realized baseball might be within Moore's range of erudition and gasped, "Why?"

"I've read his instructive book on the art of pitching," Moore said. "and it's a pleasure to note how unerringly his execution supports his theories."

While being a renowned poet, Moore went on to become a loyal fan of the Brooklyn Dodgers in the days of Roy Campanella, Don Newcombe, and the boys of summer Roger Kahn glorified in his famous book. She wrote poems about baseball, one she called *Baseball And Writing,* which begins:

> *Fantacism? No. Writing is exciting*
> *And baseball is like writing*
> *You can never tell with either*
> *How it will go*
> *Or what you will do*

Moore's assertion that baseball is like writing is a curious thought. Perhaps it explains the attraction baseball has for the best writers. In *Take Time For Paradise* A. Bartlett Giamatti explains it as serendipity. "Serendipity is the essence of both games, the writing one and the baseball one," he wrote. Serendipity, of course, is fortune *and* good luck, a providence to be gained through good work but with chance having a play in it. The word fits baseball perfectly. Serendipity is at the heart of every baseball game. Line drives *and* bad hops. And, according to Giamatti, writing, too.

Baseball's most famous poem is *Casey At The Bat*, written by Ernest Lawrence Thayer in 1888. However, a hundred years before Casey there was this:

> *The Ball once struck off*
> *Away flies the Boy*
> *To the destin'd Post*
> *And then Home With Joy.*

The poet is anonymous. Whoever he or she is may have had cricket in mind when composing these lines. But what is remarkable is that they were written sometime between 1774 and 1784, long before Abner Doubleday and baseball's creation story, and despite its reference to a "post", was called *Base Ball*. Talk about serendipity. These words seemed to have materialized out of thin air.

I cite Thomas Boswell in baseball's assemblage of notable scribes if for no other reason than he and I are of similar age, affections, and home towns. We both grew up in the Washington D.C. area rooting for the Senators, a subject Boswell has written about on several occasions. In my archives I keep a copy of a *Washington Post* column he wrote about Roy Sievers, the Senator's star player in the 1950's we idolized separately. In his tribute to Sievers Boswell explained the importance of baseball heroes to young boys. They are toys of childhood and the first emotional connection boys will make outside their families. Ultimately, it will be their first experience with pain and disappointment.

W.P. Kinsella hailed from Iowa, which is where he placed most of his fiction. *Shoeless Joe* is unquestionably his most famous novel. The story it tells can be appreciated from several perspectives, one being how well baseball keeps a faithful connection with its past. Shoeless Joe Jackson was real, not imagined, and his life story is a classic tale of the fallen hero, but there is also mystery behind his downfall. Fiction can contain truths just as non-fiction can, and the truth in Kinsella's novel is that fans who honor baseball's past still question whether or not Jackson was part of the conspiracy to throw the 1919 World Series. After all, he hit .375 with 12 base hits, a Series record that lasted more than forty years.

But the novel isn't just about baseball justice or hero worshipping, The novel is about an Iowa farmer named Ray, a dreamer devoted to the game's past, who is inspired by his dreams and devotion to plow his cornfield into a ballfield so ghosts from the past can magically come back to play for their pleasure, and his. It's a ballfield in a perfect pastoral setting, with rows of corn as the outfield fence.

The power of dreams is a theme Kinsella used in other novels he wrote, like *The Iowa Baseball Confederacy*, which has a mix of the triad—pastoral setting, magic, and dreams—as strong as *Shoeless Joe*.

In *Confederacy* the main character is a baseball fan named Gideon Clark who lives with his wife Sunny in a small Iowa farm town in 1978. Gideon loves Sunny and tolerates her wanderings and occasional disappearances to muse by herself. He also has a friend Stan, a minor league player who dreams of playing in the majors someday. Gideon becomes obsessed with trying to prove there once was a minor league called the Iowa Confederacy and that in 1908 a team of its all-stars played a game against the Chicago Cubs, the best Major League team at the time.

Gideon dreams of going back in time to witness the game and prove it was real. One day, with the help of an old man named John who claims to have once played for the Confederacy, Gideon discovers a time portal on the ballfield where the game was supposedly played. With Stan accompanying him, he steps through the portal to fulfil his dream. Suddenly, it's 1908 and the Cubs are there and the game is about to begin. Stan joins the players making up the Confederacy team while Gideon poses as a sportswriter covering the game.

After nine innings the game ends in a tie, but the Cubs refuse to return to Chicago before their greatness can be confirmed with a victory and demand that the game continue. The extended play that follows becomes surreal, proceeding through 2,000 innings and weeks of play.

The President of the U.S. and Leonardo da Vinci show up to watch. The president—Teddy Roosevelt—uses his bully pulpit to pinch hit, grabbing a bat and taking a few hacks at the plate. For his part, da Vinci shows Gideon some drawings he made for the ideal layout of a baseball diamond, which amazingly matches that of the modern game.

Players die or disappear and the game continues despite a pouring rain. The statue of the Black Angel from the local cemetery shows up to play right field. As the game continues, the river rises to flood the ballfield.

During his trip back in time Gideon has met and fallen in love with Sarah, a woman from a local church. There's more than the game's outcome at stake in Kinsella's magical story and Gideon realizes his love affair with Sarah cannot end happily. The town is washed away by floodwaters. Sarah is killed in a motor car accident. The game finally ends on Day 40 with the Confederacy winning. Time travel, as it turns out, comes with a price, and when Gideon returns to present day he discovers Sunny has gone and the old ballplayer John has died.

Kinsella brought Shoeless Joe forward in time to discover truths about the past and sent Gideon backwards in time for the same reason. The pursuit of truth in a pastoral setting is a theme that connects the two stories. And maybe with a third story, too, the one about the game's creation in Cooperstown.

Kinsella's other works are baseball fairy tales, too. In his novel *Magic Time* a player with major league ambitions is assigned to play for the minor league team in the isolated farm town of Grand Mound, Nebraska. He notes a peculiarity about the town, that players who came before him never left and instead retired and stayed to take jobs, marry, and raise families. As he will discover, playing baseball in Grand Mound is just a matchmaking ruse to draw young men there to settle down and wed the town's eligible maidens, not to mention add to its work force and economy.

In Kinsella's short story *The Last Pennant Before Armageddon*, Al Tiller, the manager of the Chicago Cubs, has a recurring dream that the world will end in Biblical apocalypse if the Cubs win the pennant. On the last day of the season the Cubs hang on to first place by a thread while a potential nuclear war in the Middle East reaches a tipping point. It's the bottom of the 9th and the deciding game is tied. Several players in the dugout are listening to news on portable radios. The Cub starting pitcher Eddie Guest retires the first two batters and then walks the next two after both foul off a dozen pitches. Al is worried over what he sees: Eddie is dropping his shoulder and bending his knee too much. Meanwhile, the Cub's ace reliever Bullet Boyd is well-rested and up in the bullpen.

Al goes to the mound and asks his catcher, "How's he doin?"

"Everything but the curveball," the catcher answers. "He shoulda struck out them last two guys. They was lucky."

Kicking the dirt, Tiller thinks about his honor and duty, and the American Navy on a beachhead on the other side of the globe. Finally, patting Eddie on the shoulder, he says to him, "Don't' throw the curve."

In the bullpen, Bullet Boyd throws his glove on the ground.

"Then, honor intact," writes Kinsella, "Al Tiller slouched toward the dugout, prepared to suffer."

In *The Natural*, Bernard Malamud uses baseball to tell a modern King Arthurian fable. Instead of pulling a sword from a stone, his knightly hero Roy Hobbs carves a magical bat from the wood of a tree that was downed in a lightning storm and christens it *Wonderboy*. His name— Roy—is derived from French, meaning king. The team he plays for are the Knights. Like Sir Lancelot, Roy's excessive pride is his downfall. Like Shoeless Joe, he has a weighty moral decision to make. And like in a Greek tragedy, he must pay the price for his bad choice. "Say it ain't so, Joe," a young boy on the street reportedly said to Jackson after he had been tried and found guilty. "Say it ain't true, Roy," says the newsboy showing his hero the newspaper headline at the conclusion of *The Natural*.

"When Roy looked into the boy's eyes," Malamud writes in the book's last sentence, "he wanted to say it wasn't but couldn't, and he lifted his hands to his face and wept many bitter tears."

Have there ever been any great football writers? Has there ever been a football novel to match *The Natural* as a parable about temptation and human weakness? Nada. I know of only two football novels to speak of—Dan Jenkins' *Semi-Tough* and former NFL player Pent Gent's *North Dallas Forty*—and neither held its sport in high regard. *Semi-Tough* treated football players as superficial clowns and Gent based his novel on his experiences playing in the soulless corporate culture of the Dallas Cowboys.

Baseball has attracted other fiction writers besides Malamud. Many acclaimed novelists have leapt over the sports desk to contribute great literature to baseball's library. Mark Harris and Damon Runyon. In the *Old Man And The Sea,* Ernest Hemingway's tragic hero Santiago compares his valor to that of his idol Joe DiMaggio. And Thomas Wolfe included a story about baseball in *Of Time and the River.* So did Willie Morris in *North Toward Home.*

George Plimpton. Gay Talese. Paul Gallico.

I'm saving for another chapter in this thesis the best, Roger Angel, the dean of baseball writers.

Poets, too. Robert Frost and Carl Sandberg wrote verses about baseball.

Football fans, tell me to stop if this hurts too much.

But I have one more.

John Updike's *Hub Fans Bid Kid Adieu* is a combination of great writing and baseball history. In his famous essay Updike chronicles a Red Sox game he attended in Fenway Park in September, 1960, the last game of Ted Williams' illustrious career. Updike begins in the elegant prose that adorns all his novels. "Fenway Park, in Boston, is a lyric little bandbox of a ballpark. Everything is painted green and seems in curiously sharp focus, like the inside of an old-fashioned peeping-type Easter egg."

The Red Sox played the Baltimore Orioles that day. It was gray and gloomy, a foreboding of autumn and the season's end. Updike sat behind third base and before the game watched a groundskeeper on top of Fenway's Green Monster pick batting-practice balls out of a screen "like a mushroom gatherer seen in Wordsworthian perspective on the verge of a cliff." Updike knew baseball and went on to remind us that "of all the team sports, baseball, with its graceful intermittences of action, its immense and tranquil field sparsely settled with poised men in white, its dispassionate mathematics, seems to me best suited to accommodate, and to be ornamented by, a loner. It is essentially a lonely game."

In other words, Ted Williams was a perfect fit for the game. For over twenty years he had a love/hate affair with Boston, "a marriage composed of spats, mutual disappointments, and, toward the end, a mellowing hoard of shared memories."

A ceremony preceded the game in which speakers took turns heaping praise on Williams. Gifts were offered and received. Then Williams spoke. The small crowd in attendance—it's meager size not surprising given how terrible the Red Sox were that year—held their breathes as he began in vintage Ted. "In spite of all the terrible things that have been said about me by the knights of the keyboard up there…" He looked up at the press box behind home plate. "…and they were terrible things. I'd like to forget them, but I can't." He swallowed hard and went on. "I want to say that my years in Boston have been the greatest thing in my life."

"The crowd," wrote Updike, "like an immense sail going limp in a change in the wind, sighed with relief."

Williams was third in the batting order and drew a walk in his first at bat. He moved around the bases on subsequent walks and stood on third base in front of Updike, who described him this way. "He struck the pose of Donatello's David, the third-base bag being Goliath's head." When Red Sox batter Lou Clinton hit a fairly deep fly to center field, Williams tagged up and ran home and slid safely across the plate.

Updike noticed how Williams appeared each time he came to the plate, "pounding the dirt from his cleats, gouging a pit in the batter's box with his left foot, wringing resin out of the bat handle with his vehement grip", and realized something greater in the man than his gifts of talent: he *really* wanted to hit the ball. In the third inning he flied to deep center. In the fifth he hit a ball high and far into right field but the heavy air and a "casual" wind held it up and the right fielder caught it against the "380" sign painted on the outfield wall. On another day, in another park, Updike wrote, it may have been gone. But not today.

Williams did not bat in the sixth or seventh innings. He was second up in the eighth. Almost certainly this would be the last time he would bat in Fenway Park.

As he approached the plate, something unexpected happened. Updike wrote, "Instead of merely cheering, as we had in his three previous appearances, we stood, all of us, and applauded. I had never before heard pure applause in a ballpark. No calling. No whistling. Just an ocean of handclaps, minute after minute, burst after burst, crowding and running together in continuous succession like the pushes of surf against the sand." During it all pitcher Jack Fisher never moved. None of the Orioles did. They were frozen in position. "Only Williams had moved during the ovation, switching his bat impatiently, ignoring everything except his cherished task." Finally, with the umpire's signal to play, Fisher wound up and the applause sank into a hush.

The first pitch was a ball. On the second Williams swung mightily and missed and the crowd moaned at the sight of his classic swing bared for them. Updike shared what he was thinking at the moment.

"Understand that we were a crowd of rational people. We knew that a home run cannot be produced at will; the right pitch must be perfectly met and luck must ride with the ball. The air was soggy, the season was exhausted. Nevertheless, there will always lurk, around the corner in a pocket of our knowledge of the odds, an indefensible hope, and this was one of those times, which you now and then find in sports, when a density of expectation hangs in the air and plucks an event out of the future."

"Williams swung again, and there it was."

The ball rose on a line over center field. The centerfielder ran back to the deepest corner of the outfield grass, but the ball descended beyond his reach and landed in the bullpen, where it bounced high and then vanished. The crowd roared. Williams circled the bases as he always did for a home run, with his head down, hurriedly and unsmiling, "as if our praise were a storm of rain to get out of." The crowd noise didn't let up. Chants of "We want Ted" echoed inside the "lyric little bandbox of a ballpark" without letting up after Williams was back in the dugout.

He didn't come out again, as "our noise for some seconds passed beyond excitement into a kind of immense open anguish, a wailing, a cry to be saved". Teammates in the dugout begged Williams to go out onto the field and acknowledge the fans in some way. But he stayed put.

"Gods do not answer letters," Updike wrote.

16

Game Faces

"The sun don't shine on the same dog's ass every afternoon."
Jim "Catfish" Hunter, ex-major league pitcher
(1946-1999)

It always pleases me to see opposing players in a Major League game smiling and laughing with each another. Even in the intensity of a must-win game, they find it in themselves to remain cordial. After hitting a single a batter will chat with the first baseman while pulling off his batting his gloves like they're sharing stories about their families. For a moment cheerfulness has displaced their competitiveness. After trotting onto the field to start a game, the home team's third baseman hugs the opposing team's base coach and shakes hands with the umpire.

Football discourages fraternization. Because of its self-importance and reliance on violent collisions, football frowns on players sharing fellowship or humor during a game. Baseball welcomes it. Maybe it's because baseball players know that if they're going to survive the long season they will need to maintain an emotional balance that permits them moments of solidarity. They need to remove their game faces on occasion.

I like to think it's because baseball is a game of leisure and players are entitled to moments of leisure, too. They know the game is bigger than they are, and that allows them to be human with one another. They feel like members of a brotherhood honoring the game they respect.

In Game 6 of the 1975 World Series, considered by some to be the greatest Series game ever played, Cincinnati's Pete Rose came to the plate in the tenth inning and turned to Boston catcher Carlton Fisk to say, "This is some kind of game, isn't it?" And in the greatest *Series* ever, 1991's worst-to-first classic between the Minnesota Twins and the Atlanta Braves, Game 7 began with the Brave's leadoff hitter Lonnie Smith turning in the batter's box to shake hands with Twins' catcher Brian Harper.

Baseball lets its players laugh at themselves. Managers, too. It has a history of characters famous for humor they weren't afraid to direct at themselves. Some mixed their humor with humility.

After managing the New York Yankees to the World Series ten times between 1949 and 1961, Casey Stengel was hired to manage the crosstown Mets in their 1962 inaugural season. They lost 120 games that year and gained the reputation of perhaps being the worst team in history. Stengel tried to make light of his role in the hapless organization and one day told his barber to not cut his throat. "I may want to do that myself later," he said.

Hall Of Fame Pitcher Catfish Hunter was raised on a farm in North Carolina and retained his down-home, country mannerisms once he reached the Majors. After blowing a game for the Oakland A's in the 1972 World Series, he spoke to reporters afterwards with his game face removed. "Well, boys," he said, "the sun don't shine on the same dog's ass every afternoon."

Warren Spahn was the pitcher who gave up Willie Mays's first major league hit, a home run, after Mays had started his career going 0-for-12. Spahn told reporters afterwards, "Gentlemen, for the first 60 feet, that was a hell of a pitch." Years later, still speaking of the pitch, he added, "I'll never forgive myself. We might have gotten rid of Willie forever if I'd only struck him out."

Some players—and managers— aren't afraid of being self-effacing. Rocky Bridges, one of the Washington Senators I worshipped as a kid, was just an average shortstop playing for several teams in the American League in the 1950's. He stood five-foot-eight with stooped shoulders and the face of a smiling pit bull with a tobacco chaw in his cheek. When asked once if he had reached his full potential as a player, he replied, "I may have gone beyond it." After retiring, he become a minor league manager. "I'm a handsome, debonair, easygoing six-footer," he said at his introduction. "Anyway, that's what I told them at the Braille Institute." In a game once, his starting pitcher was getting clobbered and gave up seven runs before Bridges went to the mound. He motioned for the pitcher to hand him the ball. He examined it, turning it over, and then gave it back. "I can't believe the darned thing is still round," he said and returned to the dugout.

Football would never allow its coaches to go where Casey and Rocky lived. As generals on a battlefield they have to keep up their warlike confidence and posture. After Buddy Ryan became the Philadelphia Eagles head coach, he gave himself a grade of A+ after his first season. "I didn't make any mistakes," he said. His team had just finished 5-10-1 after going 7-9 the year before.

Football's game face is evident on the sidelines, where head coaches pace holding clipboards or play sheets in their hands and listening through headsets to battlefield advice from an assistant coach situated high in the stadium. I've never seen a coach laugh or smile at what he is being told. If his name was Tom Landry, he wore a suit and a tie. Otherwise, it's a sweater or team jacket. Baseball managers get to wear the same uniforms as their players—road uniforms, too—with numbers on their backs. So do their base coaches, who are applauded when they barehand a sharply hit foul ball and then toss it into the crowd.

Landry's game face wouldn't have been the same if he was wearing a Dallas Cowboy jersey.

Football players say boring things. They state the obvious, like, "Our goal this week is to control the line of scrimmage." Baseball players have fun saying things like, "This pitcher is so bad that when he comes in the grounds crew drags the warning track."

Baseball's lesson is *lighten up.*

Bill Lee was a Major League pitcher known for his cosmic view of everything, not just baseball. He regarded baseball as the National Pastime, but from a Bohemian point of view. It was fitting that he joined the Boston Red Sox in 1969, the year of Woodstock.

"I was ordered to report to Fenway Park," he said in an interview. "When I drove by it I took a right and a right and ended up in Cambridge and realized that when the Northwest Territories Act took effect Boston wasn't built and I couldn't find the park. When I did, and looked up at its brick façade and little red door on Yawkey Way I thought, 'This isn't a ballpark. It's a factory.' Then I walked through the gate and came down that little tunnel and all of a sudden I saw the green seats, and green wall, and the field and the proximity of the foul lines and closeness of everything and I got down on one knee (at this point in the interview Lee crossed himself) and thanked God for making me a ballplayer."

Football has never had a player like Bill Lee. The closest the sport got was Alex Karras, the lineman for the Detroit Lions known for his old fashioned, smashmouth style before retiring to become a comic actor. His playing career ended just as European-style soccer stars were arriving to take over as pro football's place-kicking, game-winners. Karras mimicked their ignorance of American football with his line, "I keeck a touchdown."

In football, specialists *kick*. In baseball, they *relieve*.

Football would have choked a player for speaking about his sport the way Bill Lee spoke about his.

"I think about the cosmic snowball theory," he said once. "A few million years from now the sun will burn out and lose its gravitational pull. The earth will turn into a giant snowball and be hurled through space. When that happens it won't matter if I get this guy out."

But then, he said this, too. "You should enter a ballpark the way you enter a church."

Lee's pitching arsenal included an *eephus* pitch, a pitch thrown with a slow, rainbow arc that is effective when the batter is surprised by it. If the batter is not surprised, well ....

The 1975 World Series is remembered for Game 6 and Pete Rose speaking to Carleton Fisk two innings before Fisk's home run won the game for Boston and forced Game 7. Few fans will remember that Lee was Boston's starter in Game 7. In the 6th inning, with Boston leading 3-0 and a runner on base for the Reds, Lee threw an eephus to Tony Perez and with a perfectly timed swing Perez launched a mammoth home run over the Green Monster that had sportswriters debating whether or not it had landed on the Massachusetts Turnpike. Cincinnati went on to win the game, 4-3, and the series.

Lee got to face Hank Aaron the year before Hammerin' Hank retired. "I'm mad at Hank Aaron for deciding to play one more season," Lee said. "I threw him his last home run and thought I'd be remembered forever. Now, I'll have to throw him another."

But Lee deserves a place in the history of baseball's arms race if only for his reply to a question he got in an interview after he had retired.

"What was your best pitch," he was asked.

"My best pitch was a strike," Lee answered with a straight face.

The interview was for Ken Burns' PBS baseball filmography released in 1994 and conducted outdoors on sunny day. Lee wore a cap that said CCCP on the crown and under its brim he squinted and smiled as he spoke. He held a baseball in his left hand, his pitching hand, that he used to demonstrate the grip, release, and spin of pitches he mentioned.

"A sinking fastball," he continued after mentioning his best pitch was a strike, "which you grip like this." He showed the camera. "So you only get two seams into it and if you turn your hand like this it curves. The wind pushes it here and forces it down and away from a right handed hitter, thereby he thinks it's a good pitch. At the last minute it sinks and he hits the top half of the ball. He hits a groundball to Burleson and Burleson picks it up and throws"—Lee pointed off-camera to his left—"to Yastrzemski. One away. You do that 27 times in the ballgame and you make 27 outs."

Lee was starting to sound like a pitching coach who was half-baked.

"Unless the hitters are smart. They know it's a sinker and they get up and drive the ball to right-center field"—he looked over his shoulder—"between Lynn and Evans and that's called a double. And then I have to run behind third base and back it up, and hopefully we get the guy out at third, or it's a triple. Now they've got a runner at third with less than two outs. So, we bring the infield in."

Where is he going with this? you wonder.

"I don't want him to hit a sinker. I have to strike him out." Then Lee paused. Squinting into the sun, with a serious game face, he finished.

"I have to go to a cross-seamed fastball, which I don't have."

17

The Fabric Of The Game

"Can I throw harder than Joe Wood? Listen, my friend, there's no man alive can throw harder than Smoky Joe Wood."

__Walter Johnson, Hall-Of-Fame pitcher

"Oh, I don't think there was ever anybody faster than Walter."

____Smoky Joe Wood

Smoky Joe Wood was a pitcher who joined the Boston Red Sox in 1908.

Born in Kansas City in 1889, he grew up in southwestern Colorado, where he recalled seeing stagecoaches pass through town carrying gold from nearby mines drawn by six horses and protected by two riflemen riding on top. In 1906 his family moved back to Kansas and he began to play baseball as an amateur for the local town team. Later that year he turned professional as one of the few male players allowed to play on an all-female barnstorming team called the Bloomer Girls.

From there he got his first big step in organized baseball signing with a team in Hutchinson, Kansas, and one year later was sold to the Kansas City team in the American Association. In the middle of his first season in Kansas City he was sold to the Red Sox. He was only 18 years old.

Wood lasted with the Red Sox until 1917. By that time he had played on three winning World Series teams alongside future Hall of Famers Tris Speaker, Harry Hooper, and another young pitcher named

Babe Ruth. Like Ruth, Wood finished his career as an outfielder, but with occasional pitching stints, too, not as Ruth's teammate with the Yankees, but as Speaker's with the Cleveland Indians.

Wood had an impressive Major League career. He went 34-5 in 1912 and was famous for one game in particular played on September 6th that year, when he faced in a much-hyped pitching duel the Washington Senator's Walter Johnson, the American League's best pitcher in the first two decades of the 20th century. Wood was not scheduled to pitch that day but the Senators challenged the Red Sox to move him up in the rotation so Wood could oppose Johnson in a matchup that would be promoted like a heavyweight prizefight. And it was. Newspapers published comparisons of the two pitchers' heights and weights, biceps, and arm spans. The hype included the fact that Johnson had just seen his record streak of 16 consecutive wins snapped while Wood's—currently at 13—was still going strong. A crowd of 29,000 packed Fenway Park for the game and fans sat on the grass just barely outside the foul lines.

Johnson and Wood battled to a scoreless tie through five innings. Then, in the sixth the Red Sox scored a run on back-to-back doubles by Speaker and Duffy Lewis. After that, Wood held the Senators scoreless to win the game, 1-0, giving up only two hits.

In 1981, 69 years after Wood vs. Johnson, Roger Angel, the dean of baseball writers, attended a college game at Yale Field in New Haven, Connecticut, that had drawn some pre-game excitement. It was a semifinal game of the NCAA northeast regional tournament, with the winner advancing to the College World Series in Omaha later in the month.

Angel wrote an essay titled *The Web Of The Game* in which he described the game he saw that day. The first semifinal game had already been played, in which Maine beat Central Michigan, 10-2. The second game, the one that attracted Angel, pitted Yale against St. John's University.

Angel brought a guest with him to the game, an old man who had been the Yale coach for 19 years but possessed other baseball milestones in his life as well. "St. John's has always had a good club," the guest said to Angel. "Even back when my sons were playing ball, it was a good ball team. But not as good as this one. Oh, my! Did you see the catcher throw down to second? Did you see that? I bet you in all the years I was here I didn't have twenty fellows who could throw."

In his essay Angel recalled the old man taking out his pocket watch and snapping it open. Three-fourteen. "Can't they get this started?" he said impatiently. He handed the watch to Angel. "I've had that watch for sixty-eight years," he said. "I always carried it in my vest pocket, back when we wore vests."

Angel turned the watch over and read the inscription on the back, a bit worn, but still legible.

PRESENTED TO JOE WOOD BY HIS FRIEND A.E. SMITH IN APPRECIATION OF HIS SPLENDID PITCHING WHICH BROUGHT THE WORLD'S CHAMPIONSHIP TO BOSTON IN 1912

Angel wrote that, next to Walter Johnson, "Smoky Joe Wood was the most famous fast baller of his era. Still is, no doubt, in the minds of the few surviving fans who saw him at his best. He is ninety-one years old."

He confessed how hesitant he had been inviting Wood to be his guest at the game. Angel badly wanted to meet Wood but didn't want to intrude on his privacy. The fact that the game pitted St. John's against Yale, where Wood had coached, wasn't enough.

Then, the starting pitchers were announced: Ron Darling and Frank Viola, a match-up of two of college baseball's best pitchers that year, both juniors with Major League careers in their futures. Darling, a right-handed fast baller for Yale, was 9-3 with a 2.42 ERA and 89 strikeouts in 93 innings, and would have been regarded by big league scouts as the finest college pitcher in the Northeast if not for Viola, a left-handed curve baller who was undefeated for St. John's, 9-0, with a 1.00 ERA. The pitching duel was reason enough for Angel to ask Wood if he'd like to see the game with him.

Angel recalled that Wood spoke slowly and with care, the same as he walked. He used a cane to get to his seat. There was nothing ailing about him, but he didn't move hurriedly or sprightly either. "What kind of pitcher were you, Mr. Wood?" Angel asked.

"Strictly curve and fastball," Wood replied. He confessed modestly that he wasn't smart enough to slow up his pitches. His fastball had a hop to it, which only happens when a pitcher throws *really fast.*

The game on the field had begun. Darling was throwing popping fastballs that he mixed with a deadly down-breaking slider and an occasional curve. He threw without any signs of strain. By the fourth inning he was imposing his will on St. John's batters. Frank Viola, lanky, lefty, and sharp-shouldered, threw with an assortment of spins and speeds, and sinkers and down-darting sliders that had Yale batters swinging from their shoe tops. After five innings the game was still scoreless.

"What was the score of that game you beat Walter Johnson in?" Wood was asked.

"We won, 1-0. But it wasn't Johnson's fault. If he'd had the team behind him that I did, he'd have set every kind of record in baseball."

"Were you faster than he was?" Angel asked.

"Oh, I don't think there was ever anybody faster than Walter."

'But Johnson said just the opposite. He said no one was faster than you."

"He was just that kind of fellow, to say something like that. The way he threw the ball, the only reason anybody ever got even a foul off him was because everybody in the league knew he'd never come inside on a batter. Walter was a prince of men, a gentleman first, last, and always."

A prince of men. Angel smiled at Wood's choice of phrase. Not only could an argument be made whether Wood or Johnson was the fastest, but another could be over who was most gentlemanly and modest.

After beating Johnson in the famous 1912 game, Wood went on to win sixteen in a row, tying Johnson's record.

In 1913, Wood threw out his arm in a game against Detroit at Fenway Park. He went to field a swinging bunt down the line and slipped on the wet grass and landed on his hand, suffering a minor break. He rushed his return to the lineup and came back too soon. "You have to understand," he told Angel, "that in those days if you didn't work, you didn't get paid. We had to play, ready or not." As a consequence of his haste, his shoulder went bad and his fastball lost its hop.

"Did you become a different kind of pitcher after you hurt your arm?"

"No, I still pitched the fastball."

"But the pain—"

"I tried not to think about it," Wood remembered. "I just loved to be out there."

The game before them was in the 7th inning. The Yale second baseman leaped high to catch a line drive and then flipped the ball to second to double up a St. John's baserunner and end the inning. The game was still scoreless. Darling hadn't given up a hit.

Angel asked Joe Wood if Darling reminded him of Carl Hubbell on the mound. "The way he picks up his front leg, I mean. You remember how Hubbell would go way up on the stretch and then drop his hands down by his ankles before he threw the ball?"

Wood shook his head. "To me, this pitcher's a little like that fellow Eckersley."

"How do today's players compare with the men you played with, Mr. Wood?" Angel asked.

"I'd rather not answer that question."

The game moved into the 8th, still scoreless. In the 9th the Yale leftfielder led off with a single but the next batter, attempting to sacrifice, bunted into a force play at second and a possible rally ended. Darling and Viola were matching each other in calmness, intent, and control of their pitches. Darling looked as fast in the 9th and 10th innings as he had earlier in the game. Viola was dominant in his own way, setting down Yale batters with a handful of pitches and a rhythm that had batters leaning in and out.

With two out in the top of the 11th, a St. John batter hit a slow roller up the first base line. The first baseman allowed the ball to carom off his mitt, but the second baseman raced in to snatch it and flip it in desperation toward Darling as he sprinted to cover the base. Darling grabbed the toss diving full-length at the bag and rolled in the dirt after beating the runner by a hair.

"Oh, my," said Wood. "Oh, my. Oh, my."

In the bottom of the inning Viola was missing the corners and Yale loaded the bases on a single and two walks. With two outs, the Yale batter bounced gently to short for a force that ended the inning.

In the top of the 12th St. John's leadoff hitter, Steve Scala, got a piece of Darling's first pitch with the handle of his bat and looped it over the shortstop's head for a hit, St. John's first of the game. An announcement was made that Darling's eleven innings of no-hit pitching had set an NCAA record and the crowd—including St, John's players—stood and applauded Darling's performance.

Everyone was barely seated again when Scala stole second. Then he stole third. With one out, a batter reached on an error without Scala scoring. Runners were at the corners. Darling fanned the next batter, his fifteenth strikeout in the game. There were two outs.

A pinch-runner was sent to first base and took off for second on Darling's next pitch. The catcher fired the ball quickly intending for Darling to cut off his throw. But Darling had fallen away from the mound with his follow-through and couldn't reach it and the catcher's throw passed through to second base. Scala came part way down the third baseline and stopped, while the pinch runner jammed on his brakes, too, in hope of getting caught in a rundown while Scala could scamper home. The Yale second baseman had taken the catcher's throw and he glanced at Scala before making a run at the hung-up pinch runner. When he threw to first, Scala broke for home. With the hung-up runner barely out of his reach, the first baseman hesitated too long before turning to throw home, and when he did Scala slid past the tag and came up leaping and clapping into his teammates' arms.

After eleven innings, someone had finally scored. The game was 1-0.

Darling struck out the last man, his sixteenth.

A right-handed reliever came in for St. John's in the bottom of the 12th and mowed down Yale batters one-two-three to seal the win for St. John's.

"Well, that's a shame," Joe Wood said, getting up from his seat. "If that man scores from third before the third out, it counts, you know. That's why it worked. I never saw a better-played game, college or big league. That was a swell ballgame."

St. John's lost to Maine in the final game of the playoffs and didn't advance to the College World Series. Arizona State won the title that year. Not long after his loss to St. John's, Ron Darling was selected by the Texas Rangers in the amateur draft, the 9th player chosen overall. Frank Viola was selected 37th by the Minnesota Twins, their first pick. The New York Mets acquired Darling in a trade in 1982 and with the Mets he had an illustrious career that included a World Series appearance in 1986. Viola became the winningest pitcher in the majors over the five year span between 1984 and 1988 and pitched in the World Series in 1987 for the Twins. He won the Cy Young award the following year for his 24-7 record.

In 1984, Joe Wood appeared and received a standing ovation on Old Timers Day at Fenway Park, 72 years after his memorable season and duel with Walter Johnson. On January 3, 1985, Yale President A. Bartlett Giamatti presented him with an honorary degree of Doctor of Humane Letters. Wood was 95 at the time and received the honor at his home close to the Yale ball field. He was the first big league player to be given an honorary degree by Yale. He and Cole Porter are the only two men so honored by the university.

He died six months later in West Haven, Connecticut.

Baseball doesn't forget its past. It is kept alive on a timeless continuum, a fabric where its history of players, games, and events are woven together. Again and again we keep rolling it out. Smoky Joe Wood versus Walter Johnson. Ron Darling versus Frank Viola. The games were sixty-nine years apart but in the fabric of baseball we see them side by side as timeless treasures.

We're always reaching back into baseball's history and pulling the past forward. Ron Darling probably knew all about Walter Johnson's 1-0 loss to Joe Wood in 1912. And most likely he learned that Wood was in attendance to witness his heartbreaking 1-0 loss to Frank Viola in 1981. He would have marveled at how Wood was the thread connecting the two games and thought that he too someday might be invited to watch two young pitchers with promising futures go at it in a "swell ballgame", and with that their names and his would be added to baseball's fabric.

18

Triples

"I can't tell a lie, Angela," Luke said. "There just ain't nothin' like it.

—Philip Roth, from *The Great American Novel*

I n his wickedly satiric novel *The Great American Novel* Philip Roth created a fable about a fictional baseball league filled with an assortment of comic characters. One is Angela Whittling Trust, a wealthy widow and team owner, and a casual seductress whose paramour de jour is Luke Gofannon, one of her team's star players. Luke is stoic, illiterate, and unemotional toward Angela, but that doesn't stop her from desperately trying to win his love. His heart clearly belongs to baseball yet she succeeds in getting him to admit he loves her more than a stolen base, a home run, or a fastball letter-high and a little tight. But not a triple.

"Don't get me wrong, Angela," he says, "I ain't bad-mouthin' the home run and them what hits 'em, me included. But smack a home run and that's it, it's all over."

"And a triple?" she asks.

The two of them are lying in bed together after a roll in the hay. Luke proceeds to explain what is so great about a triple.

"Smackin' it, first off. Off the wall, up the alley, down the line, however it goes, it goes with that there crack. Then runnin' like blazes. Round first and into second, and the coach down there cryin' out to ya', 'Keep comin''. So, now ya' make the turn at second, and ya' head for third, and now ya' know that throw is comin', ya' know it's right on your tail. So, ya' slide. Legs. Arms. Dust. Then ya' hear the ump, 'Safe!'

Only that ain't all. The best part, in a way. Standin' up. Dustin' off y'r breeches and standin' up there on the bag."

Angela isn't ready to give up. In the long night that follows she treats him to frequent tastes of her most passionate self. When Luke is weak and dazed with pleasure in the morning, she asks him one more time, "Whom do you love more now, your triples or your Angela Whittling Trust?"

While Luke is thinking that one through, she prays. *It has to be me. I am flesh. I am blood. I need. I want. I age. Someday, I will even die. Oh Luke, a triple isn't even a person—it's a thing.*

But the thing it was. "I can't tell a lie, Angela," Luke says. "There just ain't nothin' like it."

A triple has been called the most exciting twelve seconds in sports. It is far more exciting than a home run, which is an explosion of noise after which the batter circles the bases and disappears in the dugout. A triple is everything Luke Gofannon says it is, and more.

It is a play that can't be captured on a TV screen. It has to be seen in person, with the entire playing field in view all at once. Besides the batter wheeling around the bases, there's the outfielder chasing the ball in a foul corner or against the outfield wall. An infielder running out to receive his throw. The pitcher backing up third. The third base coach signaling the runner to slide. A viewer can't see all this on TV. No TV screen is wide enough or can be split enough to show all these parts of the play going on at once.

A triple may be thrilling but it is rare these days. A hundred years ago, when teams played 154-game schedules, there were close to 1,400 triples hit in a season. That's more than one per game. Today, even with the longer schedule, there are 50% less. Ty Cobb hit 295 in his 23-year-career and in four seasons hit 20 or more. He had a teammate, Sam Crawford, who hit 304 in his career. The all-time record for triples in a season is 36 set in 1911 by Pittsburgh's Owen Wilson. Last year, Kansas City's Bobby Witt Jr. of the Royals led the majors with 11.

Why are triples becoming extinct? Where have they gone? The late sportswriter Jim Murray once wrote, "Willie Mays' glove is where triples go to die."

But seriously.

Ballparks have gotten smaller, so while hitting a home run is easier, hitting a triple is harder. It was 483 feet to centerfield in the old Polo Grounds, 466 ft in old Yankee Stadium, and 457 feet in Pittsburgh's Forbes Field where Owen Wilson played. What's more, ballparks are closer to being round today without the nooks, crannies, and oblique angles in outfield walls that allowed a baseball to ricochet unpredictably like a pinball. Think of the V-shaped centerfield wall in Fenway Park, or how old Tiger Stadium was almost square with a 90-degree bend in the centerfield wall 440 feet from home plate. Parks that invite triples are far fewer today.

Compared to the 1970's, when artificial turf was in vogue, ballparks are mostly grass now. Grass slows hits in the outfield gaps, making it less likely they'll scoot between outfielders and reach the walls with triple possibilities.

Analytics today teach players there is little to gain trying to stretch a double into a triple—the risk isn't worth it—and it has always been gospel that making the first or third out of an inning at third base is a sin. Few players have incentive clauses in their contracts for hitting triples. Davey Johnson of the Baltimore Orioles once hit what his teammates thought was going to be a sure triple only to be surprised when Davey pulled up at second. When asked why, Davy replied, "I've got a doubles clause."

Shoeless Joe Jackson may have been Roth's inspiration for Luke Gofannon. He hit lots of triples, enough to inspire a poem.

> *Jackson, Joe, was a dashing young beau,*
> *And a slashing young beau was he:*
> *He larupped to left, and he hammered to right,*
> *Both of them good for three.*

Jackson was known to be illiterate and once during a game was taunted by a large woman seated near third base. With Jackson at bat, she ragged him with, "Hey, Jackson! Can you spell Mississippi?" She repeated it. "Can you spell Mississippi?" She wouldn't let up. Jackson then ripped a liner into the outfield gap and raced around the bases and slid into third. Dusting himself off, he hollered to the woman, "Hey, fat lady! Can you spell triple?"

19

October, 1967

When I was in college, every student at Duke was required to take two years of English Composition. It was imperative that students learn to write, even engineering majors like me. This was not an elective option and I grudgingly accepted English Comp on my class list as a first-semester freshman. And because English Comp class assignments for freshmen were pre-arranged before they arrived on campus, I was given no choice with regards to my professor or class day or time of day. I was assigned to a class taught by Wallace Jackson that met every Monday, Wednesday, and Friday during 5th period.

I didn't see the need for English Comp in my engineering education and my first impression of Wallace Jackson did nothing to improve my attitude about the course or its irrelevance to engineering. He was not a professor I could relate to. In class he wore soft-sided shoes and a corduroy jacket with patches on the elbows, and lectured while peering over the top of reading glasses perched low on his nose. In delicate movements he lectured pacing in front of a blackboard and smoking cigarettes from a long, thin black holder. In daydreams I missed most of what his lectures could teach me.

At our inaugural class, Jackson laid out his plan for the semester. We would write a paper a week. In addition to 3 hours of classroom lectures, we would attend weekly private sessions with him in his office, one-on-one for a half-hour, while he graded our paper for that week. I viewed this as excessive punishment, with the only consolation being I got to pick the day and time of my individual sessions. So as to not break into my valuable gym time, I chose Mondays at 9:30 AM.

When I was 18, writing held no particular interest for me. A paper a week—and thirty minutes in Jackson's office while it was being graded—would go down like medicine. Regrettably, the attitude adjustment I needed in order for his class to have any meaning for me at all would not come in time.

Every Monday after 1st period Calculus I rode a bus to the women's campus and walked to the two-story music building tucked in a wooded corner of the campus, where Jackson's office was. Being fall semester, the campus was yellow and golden brown and I kicked up dry leaves as I walked across the wide lawn to the music building. The inside of the building was a charming mix of high ceilings and creaking wood floors and the muted sounds of instruments being played behind paneled doors. The building's ancient, dark halls were not unpleasant, but each week as I climbed the back stairs to Jackson's office a queasiness twisted my stomach. I wasn't looking forward to the half-hour ahead. I remember the inside of his office as being bright with sunshine, with tall windows that overlooked the campus outside, and shelves of books extending to the ceiling on the other three walls. Jackson sat behind a desk at the bottom of a well of books.

The routine each week was the same. I would sit in a chair next to Jackson's desk for ten minutes or so while he graded the paper I had written the night before. I received mostly C's, the result of an uninspired mind that preferred to be doing something else.

Jackson couldn't be blamed for my mediocrity. Far from it, he tried to inspire me. The intent of the private sessions became evident—or should have—after the grading was done. It wasn't about the paper. The balance of the session was for something else: conversation, engagement, and a search for my passions and ideas to write about. But none of this was clear to me at the time. Jackson had an agenda for the sessions, which was to build a relationship with me and learn more about me. I believe he wished to draw to my numb surface some sense for the things that were important to me; to challenge me to find meaning in them; and then to be so enlightened by the meaning that I would want to write about them. It was the heart of the writing experience, the purpose of English Comp. After all, he gave his students great freedom to choose what to write about. He never graded on the basis of subject chosen, but on what we did with it, and the private sessions were his opportunity to learn the inspiration behind our choice of subjects. But in the middle of those sessions so many years ago none of this was obvious to me. His attempts to get me to talk about myself and my passions were unsuccessful. I failed him. Instead of listening and engaging with Jackson, I heard only the slow ticking of the clock on the wall.

He almost connected with baseball.

It was October, 1967, and the World Series was underway. It wasn't just any World Series but the great autumn classic that pitted Bob Gibson's Cardinals against Carl Yastrzemski's Red Sox, and the Red Sox had battled three other American League teams to win the pennant on the last day of the season to get there. When a brief remark he made about the series drew a sparkle in my eye, he sensed he might be close to my soul and pressed on, sharing a piece of his own life about growing up in New York.

Jackson had been a New York Giants fan. He watched Willie Mays play at the Polo Grounds. It was a story he started but didn't finish; it was meant to be a seed to get *me* started. He had invited me to his office to talk about myself, not listen to him. Now he was inviting me into his life, too.

But I gave him nothing in return. I should have been curious. I should have asked him if he had been at the first game of the 1954 World Series, the game in which Mays made *the Catch*, an astonishing over-the-shoulder grab of Vic Wertz's flyball to the deepest part of the Polo Grounds. I should have asked how he felt when the Giants abandoned New York to move to San Francisco. If Mays had been his idol, I could have told him about mine, Roy Sievers of the Senators. But we had only clips of chatter. And silence. Me and Yastrzemski. We both failed that fall.

One day I came around to recognizing his intended purpose, but sadly too late. One day I came to regret the opportunity lost in 1967. Later still, I discovered my own personal love for writing. And I developed a fondness for reading the good writing of others, and figuring out what made it good, and trying to be a good writer myself. I acquired a love for baseball writing. For the simple pleasure of it, not as a class assignment, I sought to read the books of good baseball writers, like those who saw Willie Mays play in the Polo Grounds. Wallace Jackson could have been W. P. Kinsella. With baseball, we may have shared equal devotions. I could've written about the Red Sox and Yaz's incredible season. Jackson would have welcomed it.

But in 1967 my mind was closed to such possibilities.

Every spring, at the end of the academic year, Duke students voted for their favorite professors. That year I learned Wallace Jackson was a perennial favorite in the English department. In the same halls where Reynolds Price and William Styron had taught, Jackson was considered one of the best. Most likely, down those halls wandered English majors who would have begged for 30 minutes of their favorite professor's undivided attention. Through dumb luck, an undeserving freshman with little appreciation for English Lit was granted 7 hours alone with him that semester, time that was wasted. I regret it to this day. But, if those events in 1967 are still so important to me that I want to write about them now, maybe the time wasn't wasted after all. It just took me a long time to figure it out.

Yaz, (or, The Paper I Should Have Written in October, 1967)

As the curtain came down on this past summer, I was in northern New Hampshire with Henry, the father of a high school friend, backpacking in the White Mountains. For several days we hiked on a high treeless ridge where the mountains are named after presidents, drawing water from springs and carrying everything we needed, including enough food for several days, and sleeping on the ground under the stars.

Henry and I awoke on our last day to snow flurries and a hard north wind. We packed up and hiked over rocks through dense clouds until we came to a trailside hut where we took temporary shelter. The hut was a small building with a bunkroom, kitchen, and dining room perched on the edge of a mountain face several thousand feet above the valley below and staffed to meet the needs of hikers seeking companionship, a bunk for the night, or just the warmth of a wood stove. While Henry and I sat inside drying out, the cook in the kitchen had a radio on. He was listening to a baseball game. I recognized the voice of Ken Coleman, the play-by-play broadcaster of the Boston Red Sox.

My ears perked up to the game I knew Ken was describing. It was an important game for sure. Major League baseball was treating its fans to a memorable season as four teams in the American League—Chicago, Minnesota, Detroit, and Boston—battled for the pennant in the tightest race in history. Each day of the past several weeks had ended with a different order in their standings. For fans in New England, the pennant race was a rare thrill; their beloved Red Sox had finished last the year before and had not won a pennant in 21 years.

For days I had been out of touch with the world beyond the mountains and its breaking news. But that day in a remote trailside hut, far from life's comforts and routines I had connected with a distant sporting event via a radio signal. Ken Coleman was dispatching baseball news to the distant corners of New England as Paul Revere of the airwaves. I felt connected to the world again.

After warming for an hour, Henry and I left the hut and started down the mountain on a trail sheltered from the wind in a thick forest. We met other hikers going up. One of them surprised me with the question, "Know how the Sox are doing?" It was as if the answer could only be found on Mount Madison, the mountain Henry and I were descending, sort of like asking, "How's the view on top?" I was glad to share what little I knew.

"They're up 2 to 1 in the fifth," I said.

And then a second question. "How's Yaz doing?"

Simply Yaz.

Carl Yastrzemski was Boston's left-fielder. He had inherited the position seven years before from the retiring Ted Williams, who had owned it since 1939. Yaz was earning his own place of glory in Red Sox history that year, entertaining Boston fans with an astonishing show of clutch hitting that would earn him the triple crown, baseball's trifecta of leading the league in average, home runs, and runs batted in. If the season ended that day, with still a month to go, he was a lock for the most valuable player award. But there was a pennant race to win and ahead lay the race's most grueling month.

We didn't know it then but Carl's best was yet to come. In September he would elevate his game to an even higher plane and treat baseball fans to the greatest individual single-month performance ever, and he was starting that day, the day Henry and I descended Mount Madison.

I continued to follow the race after I got home—and after I left for college. In the next two weeks Yaz went 23-for-44 with five home runs, singlehandedly keeping the Red Sox in the four-team race. With two weeks to go they shared first place with the Twins and Tigers, but the White Sox swept a three-game weekend series with the Twins while Boston lost three straight to Baltimore. On Monday Detroit led the White Sox by a half game, and the Twins and Red Sox by one. Then the Red Sox took two from Detroit, with Yaz homering as the Sox won the first game, 6-5.

It appeared no one wanted the pennant. Or they all did. The four teams were stumbling over each other to the finish line. Then, with six days to go, Chicago lost a couple games to the lowly Senators and fell out of the race.

The remaining three teams entered the last weekend of the season with Boston a game behind both Minnesota and Detroit. The Tigers were at home playing back-to-back doubleheaders against the Angels, while the Twins and the Red Sox would play each other in single games on Saturday and Sunday in Boston. To win the pennant, the Sox needed to sweep the Twins and the Tigers had to lose 3 of its 4 games.

On Saturday Yaz singled in the 5th inning to give Boston a 2-1 lead and then hit a 3-run homer in the 7th to secure a 6-4 Red Sox win. Surprisingly, Detroit lost both its games. With one day left all three teams were still in the race.

On Sunday the Twins took an early 2-0 lead and held it for several innings. The Fenway Park scoreboard reported that Detroit was ahead of the Angels in their first game.

With the bases loaded in the 6th inning, Yaz singled to drive in two runs and tie the game. The Sox went on to score three more before the inning was over. With the Sox leading 5-2 in the 8th, the Twins had two runners on base with two outs when Bob Allison lined a hit to Yaz in left field. After an instant in which he considered throwing home, he threw a strike to second baseman Mike Andrews instead to cut down the sliding Allison as he tried to stretch his hit into a double. Inning over. The Sox went on to win, 5-3. Yaz had gone 4-for-4.

An agonizing wait began. The Tigers had won their first game and if they won the second, the two teams would meet in Boston the next day for a single-game playoff. In the Red Sox clubhouse players sat around a radio listening as the Tigers, trailing 8-5 in the 9th inning, loaded the bases with one out. Suddenly, there was a groundball and when the announcer said "…and over to first, in time for the out," the clubhouse exploded in celebration. Finally, the wildest pennant race ever was over. The Sox were going to the World Series.

I followed the progress of both games on a TV in the commons room of my college dorm.

When the two games were over. I had a daydream. I imagined I was in a trailside hut listening to Ken Coleman on a radio dispatching news of Boston's last game across a range of presidents in the White Mountains. In my daydream I stayed at the hut until the game was over. I pictured myself leaving and descending Mount Madison and being stopped by hikers going up. One asked me, "Didja hear any news about the Sox?"

"They did it. They won."

"Great. And Yaz? How'd he do?"

"Four-for four. He did it again."

The Perfect Game

"It's the story that counts. Once it's been told, it's as good as true."

——W.P. Kinsella, from *The Iowa Baseball Confederacy*

The most famous comedy routine of all time was about baseball. Written and first performed on stage sometime around 1932, Abbott and Costello's *Who's On First* sketch was introduced to a national radio audience in 1938 on the Kate Smith Hour. Two years later they performed an abbreviated version in a movie called *One Night In The Tropics* to such high acclaim they got their own contracts for movies that included the entire routine. Over the years they performed it hundreds of times for live audiences, including once for President Roosevelt. The routine became a national heirloom and a copy can be found in the Library of Congress. Another is in the Baseball Hall of Fame in Cooperstown.

The routine appeals to both baseball fans and those who mock baseball fans for being so obsessive about their sport's distinctions. But there never could have been a football routine like it, could there? What would it have been called? *Who's At Right Tackle?*

Baseball's position players are permanent fixtures on the field. They represent something lasting in a moving, everchanging world. They are unfailingly there for us. This adds comic irony to a routine that gives players at certain positions uncertain names like *who, what, why,* and *I don't know.*

The sketch starts with Abbott reminding his partner about the funny names of real baseball players, Dizzy and Daffy Dean, pitchers for the St. Louis Cardinals at the time. In his essay *99 Reasons Why Baseball Is Better Than Football,* Thomas Bowell wrote about nicknames. "Baseball has Blue Moon, Catfish, Spaceman, and the Sugar Bear. Football has Lester The Molester, Too Mean, and the Assassin." It's Reason No. 6 on Thomas's list.

This thesis has cited a variety of reasons why baseball is our greatest game. Besides being a perfect game that is fun to watch, baseball is like life. It follows the seasons and rhythms in our lives and reflects how we live and what we value. It's in our History, Literature, Religion, Culture, and Shared Leisure. I capitalize these five subjects because they sound like the class list for a college semester. They could be the required courses for a Baseball Major.

To the list we could add comedy.

Baseball is the only team game in which players perform on their own. They are free to act independently while serving the good of the team. When called for, players will *sacrifice* their independence for the team. This balance between individual freedom and service to the common good also happens to be our nation's ideal and is found at the core of the Constitution we swear allegiance to. We are asked to be *fair* with one another, and why shouldn't we when the baseball nation is blanketed with fairness? The fair territory of every ballfield is infinite, extending beyond its outfield fence to meet and overlap with the fair territories of other ballfields, until the entire country is fair without a single space getting missed as foul.

"We do this every day," said Orioles manager Earl Weaver. Playing every day is baseball's blessing. It makes pennant races exciting and gives fans the thrill of following them day-to-day until a winner is decided. No other sport has anything to compare with baseball's pennant race. Football has never ended a season with excitement that can match the American League's last day in October, 1967.

The Football Hall of Fame is located beside a freeway in Canton, Ohio. Canton was chosen because in 1920 its citizens launched a well-organized campaign to gain the city's designation as the birthplace of American football. Was the game invented there? No, but Canton was the founding site for the American Professional Football Association, which became the NFL we know today. Canton has a history that can't be denied. It contains no myths. Basketball's Hall of Fame also sits beside a freeway, in Springfield, Massachusetts, chosen for historical reasons, too. It was where a college physical education teacher devised the game in 1891 so baseball and football players had a game to play in the winter to stay in shape.

Cooperstown was selected for Baseball's Hall Of Fame because of a myth. Because the story is a myth, there is no recorded history of what happened that day Abner Doubleday supposedly invented the game that became the National Pastime. But I submit that *because* of the myth Cooperstown is the best site for the Hall. The myth—that is, baseball's creation story—gives us the *ideal* of baseball. In its illusion we can imagine what the game on creation day would have been like, starting with the pastoral setting Cooperstown offers, a landscape of green pastures and open spaces and distant rolling hills, clouds rising above the horizon, and the town nestled beside a lake, not a freeway, away from the noise and commotion of a big city. The myth brings the game close to us, as a place of *leisure.* The ballfield in our illusion is like the one we find in small towns today, with players competing with a combination of intensity and grace in front of people they know. It's *shared* leisure. In the quiet peace we hear the sounds of the game, the chatter of the players, the thump of pitches striking the catcher's glove, and the crack of a hit ball. We embrace the illusion and keep it alive in stories we tell. That makes it true. It's the story that counts, and once it's been told, it's as good as true.

In the 1954 World Series, Willie Mays made "The Catch", a moment of baseball glory that can be found on its continuum. At the time it was considered the most astounding catch of a flyball fans had ever seen.

Here's the story of The Catch.

It was Game 1 of the World Series, played between the New York Giants and the Cleveland Indians in the Polo Grounds. The score was tied 2-2 in the 8th inning and Cleveland had two runners on 1st and 2nd with one out. Slugger Vic Wertz was at the plate. Wertz smashed a high flyball to the deepest part of centerfield where the outfield wall was 483 feet from home plate. From his shallow position in center, Mays turned at the crack of the bat and raced after it. No fan in attendance watching the flight of the ball thought he could track it down, much less catch it. But Mays kept running until he was in a place where no other player had ever gone before and reached up to make an over-the-shoulder catch, and as he was turning and falling at the same time he threw back to the infield to prevent the runners from advancing. Spirited by Mays' astounding catch, the Giants went on to win the game 5-2 in extra innings and sweep the Series.

A sportswriter in attendance said of Mays' Catch, "That ball would have gone out of any other park in America, including Yellowstone."

There's comedy in the story. The Giant's pitcher was Don Liddle, a left hander who had been called in from the bullpen to face only one batter, the left-handed Wertz. After Mays's catch—the second out of the inning—Giant manager Leo Durocher went to the mound to replace Liddle. As Liddle handed the ball to the new pitcher, he said, "Well, I got my man."

Since then, baseball fans have seen countless catches that rival Mays'. Ken Griffey, Ichiro, Torri Hunter and many other heroes of the game have made catches that left us agape. But in our illusion of the game there has been only one Catch, and because it was an original made by an original, it has become legend. "There's heroes and there's legends," said the Babe in *The Sandlot*. "Heroes get remembered but legends never die." Mays is legendary, and so is the Catch, regarded as the greatest despite the fact there have been many great catches made by others. Mays is remembered as a possessor of the five talents. *"Well done, good and faithful servant, enter into the joy of your master."* (Matthew 25:21)

Baseball is perfect. Infields are perfect. Ninety feet has been the perfect distance between bases since the game was invented. An infield contains the perfect arrangement of lines and shapes. It's a diamond with perfectly placed circles for the mound and cutouts for the bases.

Within the perfect game, there have been perfect games.

Don Larsen of the New York Yankees pitched a perfect game in the 1956 World Series. He's the only pitcher to perform the feat of being *perfect* in a Series game, when he beat the Brooklyn Dodgers 2-0 without allowing a single runner to reach base.

"I had great control," he said after the game. "I never had that kind of control in my life." Larsen was an unlikely hero. The previous year, in the 1955 World Series, he had given up 5 runs in a game the Yankees lost

8-3 to the Dodgers, and in his first start in the '56 Series he lasted only 1-and-2/3 innings in a 13-8 loss. His lifetime career record was 81-91.

But at Yankee Stadium on September 29th, 1956, he was perfect.

His catcher that day was Yogi Berra. It could be said that Yogi *called* the perfect game. Baseball's archive contains an iconic video of Berra rushing to Larsen after the last out, bouncing and leaping into his arms in celebration. The two players are linked forever by that scene.

Forty-three years later, on June 18, 1999, before a game at Yankee Stadium Yogi was honored on Yogi Berra Day. Larsen was there and before the game threw out the first pitch to Berra from the mound. After speeches and gifts and cheers from the crowd, the pair stayed to watch the game between the Yankees and the Montreal Expos.

David Cone pitched for the Yankees that day. In the first inning two specifics of the game became clear. One was that Cone's slider moved like a wiffle ball, that is, it had *amazing* movement. Recalling the game years later, Cone described his slider as "floating like a frisbee" and his fastball "nicking the corners". The other specific was that the home plate umpire Ted Barrett was calling a generous strike zone.

Serendipity, according to Merriam-Webster is "the gift of finding valuable and agreeable things not sought for". To A. Bartlett Giamatti, it is the essence of baseball. Serendipity for a batter is when the pitcher throws him an absolutely unhittable pitch around his knees and he golfs it into the grandstands for a home run. For a pitcher, it's when he has good stuff but good fortune, too, and when he throws a mistake pitch it somehow turns into an out. It could be said that some of the serendipity that blessed Larson in 1956 was still floating in Yankee Stadium that day for Cone to pull out of the air.

In the first inning Montreal's Terry Jones hit a line drive into right-center but Paul O'Neill raced over to make a sliding catch for the out. In the third, after the Yankees had staked him to a 5-0 lead, Cone began to notice how free-swinging the Expos were behaving. "That was the scouting report," he said later. "So, I knew it was a good day to try to exploit that." He struck out the 7-8-9 hitters in the Expos' lineup on sliders that broke out of the strike zone. "They kept swinging and I kept throwing it. I threw just enough fastballs to keep them honest."

In the fifth, after Cone had retired the first 13 batters he faced, broadcaster Tim McCarver made an ill-advised remark to his TV audience, jinxing Cone by noting the coincidence of him perhaps pitching a perfect game with Don Larsen in attendance. "I mean, my gosh. What? Yogi Berra, Don Larsen—no, c'mon. That can't happen. So we just won't look for it, OK?"

In the seventh Cone induced Wilton Guerrero to hit a chopping ground ball far to the left of third baseman Scott Brosius. Shortstop Derek Jeter was well positioned to field it but too deep to throw Guerrero out, but Brosius raced far to his left and was able to cut it off with time to throw to first for the inning's first out. Three pitches later, Cone spun a frisbee slider to strike out James Mouton. Then he fanned Rondell White to end the inning. It was twenty-one batters up, twenty-one batters down.

"Call your friends," McCarver continued with his jinx remarks, "David Cone has a perfect game." In the bottom of the seventh Larsen joined him in the broadcast booth to talk about his World Series perfect game and the proper etiquette in the dugout during such a performance.

With one out in the eighth, Cone fell behind Jose Vidro, 2-0. Having no desire to be careful with Vidro, Cone took a chance throwing him a fastball down the middle of the plate. Vidro caught up with it and struck a hard grounder back up the middle which Cone—recalling later—thought immediately was a hit. But second baseman Chuck Knoblauch ranged far to his right to snare it at the edge of the outfield grass and throw Vidro out.

It was a steamy, sweaty day in New York and several times Cone had gone into the clubhouse to change tee shirts. In the tense moments before he took the mound for the ninth inning, he stared at himself in the clubhouse mirror and said, "Don't...you...dare...blow...this."

As Cone was throwing his final warm up pitch before the ninth, TV showed him on the mound on a split screen with Larsen seated in the stands. Cone always threw his last warm up from the stretch, not a wind-up. Always. He was three outs away. No changing anything now. He stretched and threw. Catcher Joe Girardi fired a strike to second base. The ball was tossed around the horn. The 9th inning began.

If there was one moment that proved serendipity was in Cone's corner that day, it was when he threw Montreal's first batter Chris Widger three straight sliders to start the ninth inning. The first one broke out of the strike zone but Widger swung and missed. Cone's second broke into the zone but Widger took it for a called strike. Then, Cone threw one that broke outside by a foot and Widger swung and missed for strike three. There was one out.

The second out was an awkward catch made by leftfielder Ricky Ledee after it appeared he had lost the ball in the sun. Then, after seeing two sliders from Cone, Orlando Cabrera popped the third one harmlessly in front of third base and as Brosius centered under it Cone, finally, *knew* he had done it.

His teammates mobbed him and carried him off the field on their shoulders. Yankee Stadium went wild. McCarver's sidekick in the broadcast booth, former-Yankee Bobby Murcer asked, "Has this been a perfect day or what?"

"Yogi Berra Day," Cone said later. "Don Larsen throwing out the first pitch. The 88 pitches. Yogi's number was 8. The random variance of things. The luck factor."

He finished with, "It's a baseball gods thing."

It's not widely known that Abbott and Costello broke up at the end of their careers. On the morning of March 3rd, 1959, as his Los Angeles Dodgers were starting their second spring training since leaving Brooklyn, Bud Abbott turned on his television set to watch an old Abbott and Costello movie. *Who's On First* was part of the movie. Near the end of the routine, his phone rang and he answered it. He was told that Lou Costello had died. "Tell me," he would often say after that, "why did I happen to be watching that picture at that time. Will you tell me?"

In their famous routine eight players on the field were named. The right fielder was never identified. *Never.* Not in hundreds of performances of the routine did the comedians tell us who was playing the position. Maybe they knew all along but didn't tell us. Maybe on that day in 1959, after learning his partner had died, Bud Abbott heard God's voice saying to him, "Don't worry. I told you I've got it."

Printed in the United States
by Baker & Taylor Publisher Services